Training a Search and Rescue Dog

for

# Wilderness Air Scent Detection

By Christy Judah

# Training a Search and Rescue Dog

## For Wilderness Air Scent Detection

Figure 1 K9 Juno.  Handler:  Beckie Stanevich.

*By Christy Judah*

# Training a Search and Rescue Dog
## For Wilderness Air Scent Detection

By Christy Judah.

ISBN-13   978-1500141967
ISBN 10   1500141968

**Front cover image:**  Search and Rescue K9 River.  Owned and handled by Tracy Sargent.  Photo by Tracy Sargent.

## Contact Information:
www.christyjudah.com                 christyjudah@gmail.com
(910) 842-4843        Brunswick County, Supply, North Carolina

## Other Books by this Author:
A Tribute to Search and Rescue Dogs
An Ancient History of Dogs:  Spaniels through the Ages
Building a Basic Foundation for Search and Rescue Dog Training
Buzzards and Butterflies:  Human Remains Detection Dogs
Water Search:  Finding Drowned Victims
Search and Rescue Canine Training Log & Journal
Search and Rescue Training Log & Journal
Building a Search and Rescue Team from the Ground Up
Training a  Human Remains Detection Dog

The Legends of Brunswick County:  Ghosts, Pirates, Indians & Colonial North Carolina
More Legends
Two Faces of Dixie:  Politicians, Plantations, and Slaves
A Journey through Sampson County
The Faircloth Family History
The Faircloth Family History-2013

Meet the Pirates
Meet the Police Dogs
Meet the Native American Indian
Meet the Search and Rescue Dogs
The English Springer Spaniel Puppy
Sabbath Home Baptist Church:  95 Years of Service
Stedman Baptist Church:  Celebrating a Centennial
The Church Journal

Published by Coastal Books.
Printed in the United States of America.

# Table of Contents

Figure 2 K9 Hope.  Handler:  Chris Holmberg.

*Our heart remembers the dogs that have crossed the Rainbow Bridge....*
*We will walk together again someday.*

Figure 3 K9 Bailey.  Handler:  Christy Judah

# Dedication

This work is dedicated to the memory of all SAR dogs that have already crossed the Rainbow Bridge, especially my Bailey, Bert's Denali, Shelly's Binka, and Jim's Storm.

Figure 4 K9 Bailey and Christy Judah.

# Forward

Training a search and rescue dog is a rewarding challenge. Being able to find a missing or lost person or help to recover the remains of a person is an experience that few share. Training those dogs takes sincere dedication, for the right reasons, consistency, efficiency, and deliberate steps. It is not something which occurs by happenstance or magically appears. It is a process which is clearly designed, applied, and documented. Just as there are innumerable ways to train an obedience, agility, hunting, or show dog, there are as many trainers with ideas on how to train a search and rescue dog, and in any process, there is no *one* right technique. There are as many recommendations for training techniques as there are trainers. This books hopes to document the technique which I have used over the years to train my and other SAR dogs in our unit in the discipline of Wilderness Air Scent. I have also cross-trained them in Human Remains Detection. It is a process that uses techniques taught to me by Bert Lark, in a variation of a back-chaining technique and incorporates a refind. It heavily relies on scent theory and is easily a basis for adding human remains detection, should the handler desire to cross-train.

The decision to pen this book evolved as a result of repeated questions by others about how I train a SAR dog. I made the decision to write this guide after multiple requests to assist in "starting" a dog for air scent or cadaver via email or in person and realized that it might be helpful to others. I hope in some small way I may assist another in continuing along the journey of training a SAR dog...a journey which never ends and continues to evolve as time passes and new information emerges. This is only one of many ways to train...adapt as you see fit, adopt as you would like, copy to share as needed, and help another to carry on the spirit of search and rescue volunteerism. It is not about "me, me, me, or my office, or my skill...it is about the missing person and bringing them back home. Keep things in perspective at all times and share your experiences and knowledge with new folks as the opportunity arises. Andy and Marcia and Susan and many others have led us to this point. I, like many others, cannot thank them enough for the foundations they laid. What they did and continue to do matters and will continue to guide many around the world.

Figure 5 K9 Gypsy. Handler: Christy Judah. Fire Rubble

# Thank You

Thank you to my Dad, Herman Faircloth, for countless hours hiding for my dogs throughout the years. At 87 years old he is still active in supporting SAR, most recently being our missing person in K9 evaluations. He retired from the United States Army with experience and missions like finding downed planes in the outback of Alaska as early as 1964, so I guess it was in the blood.

Thank you to Bert Lark and his K9 Denali, who molded me, guided me, healed my bruised ego as I trained for SAR Tech I testing, held my hand as I muddled through the early years, and who became a lifelong friend and confident. I will not soon forget his technique of asking me, "what did your dog do?" each time I completed a training assignment. He made me stop and think through each and every exercise as I learned to read my dog and understand how we communicated in the most subtle of ways. Thank you, my friend, Bert.

Thank you to Wendy Long, who has walked this search and rescue walk with me since we began in the mid 1990s. When I was frustrated or anxious, she calmed my spirit with her ever tranquil personality and demeanor. You have been my friend and confident for many years. Thank you, Wendy, for always being there to support my adventures and flank me for so many missions. And now you and K9 Beau walk that walk as you continue your SAR volunteerism in serving others and working a SAR dog. You are an inspiration.

Thank you to Shelley Wood who responded with me to many callouts...always ready, always willing, and professional. Thanks for listening all those years and continuing to be my friend and confident. Your work mattered and even in retirement, you continue to touch others.

Thank you to the law enforcement personnel, sheriffs, police chiefs, detectives, emergency managers, commissioners, and councilmen and women who have supported us throughout the years. Your support has allowed us to respond through all barriers and conditions. I will remember many of you with gratitude and a heartfelt admiration. And, oh, my gosh, thank you to all the great folks who donated their pictures to this project! It is a super contribution to this work.

Thank you to my fellow searchers and friends like Marcia, Terry, Andy, Sarah, Tracy, and Susan, literally across the globe, who have mentored, answered my questions, trained with me, guided me, supported me, and encouraged me to continue writing and searching. And to Aleta, Beckie, Bill, Carol, Gordon, Jim, Henk, Joe, Mark, Marty, Tracy, Nancy, Patti, Renee, Vi, Laurie, and so many others who have been an inspiration and friend over the years in the SAR world. Each of you touched my development and shared my experiences over the years. It mattered to me. I wish all of you the best in health and happiness.

*Christy Judah*

# Table of Photographs

*Most folks are about as happy*

*as they make up their minds to be.*

*Abraham Lincoln (1809 - 1865)*

Figure 6 K9 Grace.  Victim:  Shawn Altman.  Handler:  Lisa Altman.

Figure 7 K9 Grace.  Handler:  Lisa Altman.

Figure 8 K9 Max.  Handler:  Sherri Pharo.

Figure 9 K9 Lauren, Sit Alert.  Handler:  Christy Judah.

**Chapter One**

# Introduction to Search and Rescue

**Objectives**

*Provide an overview of search and rescue
and the job of locating missing persons.*

*List the main concepts contained in this text.*

*Provide a framework for the single- and dual-purpose dog.*

*Describe the search related skills needed by the handler
and suggestions on how to attain them.*

_____

*9-1-1…what is your emergency?*

*"I cannot find my little boy. He was just here a few minutes ago and now he is gone.
Help me…"*

*9-1-1…what is your location, sir?*

*"Please, send someone quick, I can't find my child…I need help…oh, God, help us…*

*9-1-1…an officer will be there shortly sir…*

Such is the likely beginning of a missing person case as reported to law enforcement officials. A frantic telephone call to the 9-1-1 Center or Central Communications begins the series of events which may result in a search and rescue team receiving a call from local law sheriff requesting their services; especially that of the search and rescue dog handlers.

Once requested, the handler will immediately stop whatever he is doing, change into his standard search and rescue uniform, grab his gear and his dog, and head to his vehicle. These actions begin his or her official involvement in the case; however, many hours of training, pre-planning, coordination, team functions, and trust building with first responders has taken place before this point in time. A solid foundation has been laid in personal development, search skills, canine training, and a reputation has been fostered in the SAR community before that first search mission ever happens. This book is intended to assist the canine handler build the canine training component of that foundation. Of course, handlers must recognize that the canine component is only one piece of the myriad of skills which are necessary to become a trusted, valuable and wanted canine resource in a missing person case.

Specifically, this book is designed to assist the new search and rescue dog handler to train a motivated dog in the wilderness air scent/live person detection. It is a concise step-by-step instructional manual for the handler with a good search dog candidate, carefully chosen for drive and motivation and the handler that has the dedication, time, and energy to develop this resource.

The SAR dog training described in this book *can be* expanded to add skills in locating human remains (HRD) should the handler desire to add that component; however, this book is not intended to train the single-purpose HRD dog. It also does not include any trailing or tracking training techniques. Those are very different skills sets. The singular and primary purpose of this book is to train a Wilderness Air Scent dog to locate a live missing subject.

## Chapter Overviews

The first chapter is intended to provide an introduction to SAR and recommended training background for the dog handler. It will define single and dual-purpose dogs and provide a framework for the handler to decide what his training focus will be. It will provide an overview of the specific skills needed for general search and rescue, prior to even beginning dog training and make suggestions for where to obtain that training.

The second chapter will provide information on basic scent theory. During Wilderness Air Scent training, the dog will be detecting the scent of a human being in a wilderness environment. It is essential that the handler have an understanding of basic scent theory in these applications. The third chapter will provide an overview of needed equipment and travel considerations for local, state and international missions. It will help the handler to plan for contingencies and provide suggestions for vehicle preparation.

The forth chapter will provide an overview of basic canine training or Pre-School activities that should be done prior to beginning wilderness air scent training. It will lay the groundwork for obedience, agility, socialization, and other skills needed by the typical search dog. These skills will help to prepare the dog physically and mentally for the challenges ahead.

The fifth chapter will define several types of reward systems and encourage the handler to identify and select the one which is most appropriate for their particular dog. In addition it will discuss "loyalty and focus" systems providing a choice for the handler based upon the type of training, environment or search. It will also introduce the alert, indication and final response behavior skills.

The sixth chapter will outline the stages in training a wilderness air scent dog beginning with simple "runaways" and progressing to searching 40 to 60 acre areas. It will provide a framework and curriculum to determine a level of success in preparing the dog and handler for certification testing and mission ready status.

Figure 10 K9 Binka. Handler: Shelley Wood.

Chapter seven will briefly describe and discuss cross-training the wilderness air scent dog in human remains detection. It will not provide step-by-step instructions, but will refer the reader to a companion book to train the SAR canine in human remains detection. There is a period of time when a deceased person has died and there may still be live scent in the environment. That is inevitable. However, we do not have the research or information available to become that detailed in our training techniques; therefore this book will concentrate on live scent only with tips provided later in the book regarding human remains detection. It is not within the scope of this work to determine where those boundary lines lie, but to provide training suggestions and guidelines for the air scent dog handler to recognize that we do not know if the missing person is still alive or deceased; therefore in the very least, the dog should be exposed to cadaver scent during training.

Chapter eight will describe typical crime scene preservation techniques as related to wilderness air scent. In addition, this chapter will suggest appropriate Critical Incident Stress Debriefing or CISD services which the handler may find helpful in dealing with death and other traumatic events or missions.

Chapter nine will provide a sampling of certification and evaluation testing criteria to determine whether a canine/handler team is mission ready. It will also provide hints on how to set up a valid and true wilderness air scent test should teams desire to test in-house. It will include recommendations on recordkeeping techniques, and other ethical matters related primarily to wilderness air scent canines including an introduction to courtroom testimony.

The appendix will include several sample forms for training logs, evaluation, etc. It will also include a lesson on How to Collect an Uncontaminated Scent Article should the handler desire to pursue scent discrimination training.

Throughout the book, the author has included generalized information based in reality from experience on real searches. Those vignettes help to provide thought provoking actual searches allowing the handler to begin to process techniques and lessons learned by others through experience.

## The Alive or Deceased Dilemma

The handler is not clairvoyant. He does not know if the missing person is alive or deceased. While deploying a wilderness air scent live find dog, one does presuppose that the missing person is alive. This is generally the train of thought for most first responders during the first 48 hours in a general missing person case (if there is such a thing) unless there is reason to believe the individual is already dead. In the case of an explosion or other disaster, the thought may vary. However, for the purpose of this book and the wilderness air scent training, we will suppose that the person is, in fact, alive.  However, we will also reserve the opinion that they *could* be deceased, and if so, our dog, if cross-trained and exposed to cadaver scent, will alert on the body and allow us to report his location regardless of condition. Even if not certified in HRD, the dog will present enough behaviors for the handler to recognize that something is not quite as it should be and we need to explore this more closely.  It is all about reading the dog.

A sad case clearly demonstrated this when an 11 year old boy ran into the woods after being scolded for his poor grades.  He was not actually observed entering the woods, but known to "escape" into his wilderness when upset or bothered by something.  The parents were frantic when he did not return in a timely manner and eventually called police and search teams were deployed.  A horrible scene was discovered with the boy was still holding his 22 rifle after killing himself.  He had received it as a birthday gift just two weeks prior.

Figure 11 K9 Pete.  Handler: Ben Alexander.

There is not much one can do to prepare for this sight but know that if the SAR career is long enough, there will be death scenes such as this emblazoned into your mind that are hard to erase. Luckily, most of them fade somewhat over time. Advice: Do not look at the body any more than is absolutely necessary. These images can haunt you for many years to come. Instead, look away, praise your dog, concentrate on rewarding the dog and detach yourself from the scene. If you do not protect yourself, you may become a SAR drop-out…leaving the SAR scene in short order. Your skills are too valuable to walk away too quickly. Consider CISD (Critical Incident Stress Debriefing) after such incidents. Chapter eight will acquaint you with this process more thoroughly. Suffice it to say that one never knows what you will encounter on a search – any search. Prepare your psyche for that eventual scene so that you will be able to continue your work in SAR, knowing that we have brought the missing person back to his/her family and that is our job.

Figure 12 K9 Bynn. Handler: Tracy Spilsbury.

## Single or Dual Purpose Dogs: Wilderness Air Scent and/or Human Remains Detection

Some teams and individuals use only one command to find both live and deceased victims. This book does not propose that one cannot or should not train a dog to find any human being, alive or dead, regardless of condition, with one technique or command. However, the author has found it useful to teach these two training goals as separate commands using slightly varied techniques for each and has chosen to present only wilderness air scent in this text. While impossible to train for every condition and environment, a well-trained SAR dog should have been exposed to a variety of environments, scents, and scenarios. In essence, the trained wilderness air scent dog which has been exposed to human remains can locate the missing person – alive or deceased.

Sometimes it is not practical to use one command to find either live or deceased persons, or to cross train (train a dual purpose dog) at all. In a disaster situation, when rescuers hope to find live subjects for extraction and rescue rather than spending time finding both live and deceased, only live find dogs are needed. In that environment, a dual purpose dog may put recovery resources searching for bodies instead of assisting live victims which is not the primary purpose of disaster dogs. Let it suffice to say, for the purposes of this book, the subject and training will be primarily handled as two separate training techniques which can both be taught to one search dog and used in a dual purpose dog; finding live and deceased, or taught separately for a single purpose dog— finding live subjects only or finding human remains only. Many handlers make a training decision based upon what the majority of the callout mission's warrant. They train for what the need is in their area and the number of resources in the area trained to provide those services.

Other handlers choose to train a single-purpose dog, specifically when selecting the discipline of human remains detection. With HRD, there are a myriad of additional factors to consider such as whether the training of the dog will allow the discovery to be used in obtaining warrants. This critical complication of working a human remains dog is becoming more and more of an issue in the court system. The legal issues alone concerning training a dual-purpose or single-purpose dog is a valid reason to only train a single-purpose human remains detection dog.

Handlers and trainers will need to make their own decisions regarding this matter taking into consideration the legal implications of both choices, their personal response to search requests, availability of search resources, and other factors. Study Chapter nine for more information on this topic.

Above all else, remain informed about these issues and proceed with training based upon knowledge and recommendations from your local law enforcement agencies after careful consideration.

## Terminology

Much of the terminology used in this book will be defined and attributed to the Scientific Working Group on Dog and Orthogonal Detector Guidelines (SWGDOG[1]), a national group that is designed to develop and provide consensus on the definition of commonly used detector dog terminology as defined by them in 2014. Across the United States, there is a variety of interpretation of SAR dog related terms, some varying regionally. Therefore the author has deemed the SWGDOG terminology to be the most correct use of commonly used terms and best practices in the detector dog venue.[2] Handlers should periodically check with the SWGDOG organization for updates and revisions.

## Searcher Skills

Most handlers are taught by team leaders that they are 'searchers first and handlers second.' In essence, their expertise may be needed on a particular mission even if the dog is not needed as a resource. In addition, the searcher should possess safety skills needed to ensure his and his crew's safety during the execution of a mission. He should posses good search skills to ensure the area is adequately covered and understands the basic concepts of the incident command systems. Many of these skills can be obtained by taking a Fundamentals of Search and Rescue (FUNSAR) class through the National Association of Search and Rescue[3]. Some of the topics in this class include:

1. Equipment needed to search day and night, and be self-sufficient for 48 hours.
2. Emergency survival skills in the wilderness environment.
3. Safety techniques and information.
4. Incident Command systems and forms.

---

[1] SWGDOG: Scientific Working Group on Dog and Orthogonal Detector Guidelines. http://swgdog.fiu.edu
[2] SWGDOG: Scientific Working Group on Dog and Orthogonal detector Guidelines. http://swgdog.fiu.edu/about-us/
[3] National Association of Search and Rescue. www.nasar.org

5. Clothing and person protective systems in SAR.
6. Environment hazards
7. First aid in the wilderness.
8. Travel skills
9. Land navigation skills and orienteering.
10. SAR resources.
11. Understanding self capabilities.
12. Search tactics.
13. Evidence and clue awareness.
14. Estimating POD – probability of detection.
15. Search responsibilities.
16. Tracking skills.
17. Rope and rescue equipment.
18. Radio Operations.
19. Legal aspects for searchers.

In addition FUNSAR class can improve your own personal confidence, and prepare you to begin your canine training. During the time you are training your canine, you may be responding to search missions with your team, helping to locate missing persons without the dog. Are you a valuable team asset? You should be.

It is not within the realm of this book to prepare the individual with all the needed search skills listed above. Instead, we would encourage all search personnel to take courses to gain the basic introductory skills through FUNSAR, and continue their SAR education through the years by taking courses such as Managing the Lost Person Incident, Hazardous Materials, Ropes, Advanced Search and Rescue, Cardio Pulmonary Resuscitation, First Aide, Canine First Aide, Ham Radio Operations, Air Operations, Incident Command 100, 200, 700 and 800, and a host of additional related courses. You can never learn it all and just as you have completed all the basics, things will change with additional technology and improved techniques. Continue to learn throughout your career and share your knowledge with others as you begin to mentor new recruits. Mentoring others also helps you to brush up on your own SAR knowledge. All of these experiences will only make you a better dog handler later on. Remember, searcher first – handler second. Now on to dogs...

_____

*No matter how little money and how few possessions you own,*
*having a dog makes you rich.*
*Louis Sabin.*

You are never too young or too old to learn.
Shown below is K9 Quincy, at 10 weeks of age on his first rubble pile.

Figure 13 K9 Quincy.  Handler:  Aleta Eldridge.

# Chapter Two

# Basic Scent Theory

## Objectives

*Describe the basic components which may affect the composition of human scent.*

*Provide illustrations and descriptions of some of the basic scent conditions common in wilderness environments.*

*Understand the role that scent plays in a wilderness air scent mission and how to maximize that condition for optimal dog performance.*

---

Scent is a distinctive smell. Most humans have no problems detecting the scent of lemon or garlic; a beef stew cooking on the stove top or a cake baking in the oven. They can readily identify specific perfumes and whether a scent is pleasant or not and they can discern a pleasant or not so pleasant smell in a particular threshold. (The threshold is the amount necessary for a human nose to detect the smell. In smaller amounts, the odor may not be detected by the human nose; hence a certain threshold is necessary in order for a human to detect the odor.)

A dog, on the other hand, has a much lower threshold needed to detect odors. The dog nose contains about 220 million receptors as compared to the human nose at about 5 million.[4] All we have to do is train the dog to recognize a particular odor and let us know that he has indeed found that odor. In addition, we have to place the dog in an optimum position in order for him to be able to detect that scent. In addition, we must recognize the properties of scent as they related to our work in search and rescue and

---

[4] Thornton, Kim Campbell. The 10 dog breeds with the best sense of smell. Dogtime – find your wag. November 18, 2013. http://dogtime.com/10-dog-breeds-with-the-best-sense-of-smell.html

the impacts that wind currents and other factors have upon scent detection. All of this becomes a study in scent theory.

William Syrotuk introduced scent theory in his work *Scent and the Scenting Dog*, a must read for anyone working a search and rescue dog. This provides a good overview of how scent behaves in various environments. Keeping in mind that the dog is providing his final response behavior (or trained alert) on the strongest source of the human scent and not the actual scent source itself, handlers should have a working knowledge of how scent operates and disperses in order to place the dog in the optimum location to detect odor or pinpoint the strongest odor source. This can be done with "detailing work" asking the dog to "check it" here and "check it" here, until the absolute strongest source of odor is located-usually the human being. Sometime the source with be visible and in other situations it will not. It often becomes a "trust your dog" situation with the handler simply reporting that the dog indicated the odor of a human in a specific location. However, let us not get ahead of ourselves, and take a brief look at beginning scent theory as it relates to human remains detection.

Live human scent is individualized. Cadaver scent is generic and at the time of death becomes the same for all. As the body decomposes the scent changes both physically and chemically. The decomposition is affected by microorganisms, temperature, humidity, and air. It is quite odiferous initially, but then subsides in the amount of smell recognizable by humans as time passes.

Just for the curious...Kim C. Thornton has identified her picks as the top ten breeds with the best sense of smell...and they were[5]:

1. *Bloodhound: This giant hound has 300 million scent receptors — more than any other breed. He is famed for his man-trailing abilities and is so reliable his evidence is admitted in court. Bloodhounds can not only follow a scent on the ground, they can also air scent. Like their cousin the Basset, they are built to be the perfect tracking dog, with a large, long head; a nose with large, open nostrils; long ears that sweep the scent upward from the ground; and a cape of loose skin around the head and neck to trap and retain the scent. Last but not least, the Bloodhound's stamina and persistence make him a superior trailing dog.*

2. *Basset Hound: Of French origin, the Basset is built to follow a scent trail. He's low to the ground — hence his name, from the French word bas, meaning "low" — and his long, heavy ears sweep the ground, bringing scent upward to his powerful nose. The loose skin beneath his chin, known as a dewlap, helps to trap the scent,*

---

[5] IBID.

*keeping it easily accessible as he works. According to the American Kennel Club, the Basset is second only to the Bloodhound in scenting ability.*

Figure 14 K9 Maggie. Handler: Laurie Babson. Bloodhound.

3. *Beagle: He might be one of the smallest of the hound breeds, but the Beagle has just as many scent receptors as the German Shepherd. Many of the merry little hounds follow air and ground scent. The Beagle's scenting ability makes him popular not only with hunters but also with the USDA's Animal and Plant Health Inspection Service, which employs the dogs to detect contraband (especially food items) in airports. Beagles that have been on the job for a while have a 90 percent success rate and can recognize nearly 50 distinct odors.*

4. *German Shepherd: This well-known herding breed is said to have 225 million scent receptors in his nose. One of the things he's known for is his ability to air-scent. Rather than keeping his nose to the ground, he casts about for human scent that is carried by the wind. A good German Shepherd is highly versatile, and many are employed by the police, military, and search and rescue groups.*

Figure 15 K9 River. Handler: Tracy Sargent.

5. *Labrador Retriever: The Lab is the most popular breed in the United States. Besides being a great companion dog, he is best known for his fine nose. Labs are found working in many scent-related jobs, from arson, drug and bomb detection to search and rescue.*

6. *Belgian Malinois: Commonly employed by police and military forces and as search and rescue dogs, this breed is well known for his keen sense of smell. Among the breed's talents are the ability to sniff out explosives, prostate cancer and cheetah scat.*

7. *English Springer Spaniel: This popular sporting dog comes in two types — field-bred and show-bred. Field-type Springers are highly prized by hunters for their good nose, which is liver-colored or black with broad nostrils. English Springers have been trained to detect such diverse odors as explosives, narcotics, fake currency, bee hives, and human remains. Show bred springers are also used in* search and rescue and by law enforcement agencies who recognize that their

smaller size (as compared to shepherds, labs and Malinois) make them a good candidate for detection work; especially if bred from working lines.

Figure 16 K9 Lance. Owned by Mr./Mrs. Bivens.

8. *Coonhound: The various Coonhound breeds — Black and Tan, Bluetick, English, Plott, Redbone, and Treeing Walker — all have highly effective noses but different styles of scenting. Some have "hot" noses, meaning they work best on a fresh trail, while others are said to be "cold-nosed," able to follow an old, or "cold," trail with little trouble.*

9. *German Shorthaired Pointer: Like his cousin the Pointer, the German Shorthair has outstanding scenting and trailing ability in the field. Holding his large brown nose low, he follows ground scent intensely, unlike the Pointer, who runs with his head up. A German Shorthair named Google works in Costa Rica scenting out jaguar scat to help researchers study the species.*

10. *Pointer: Hunters admire the Pointer for his bird-finding ability and say he has the best nose of all the pointing breeds. He has a long, deep muzzle with wide-open nostrils he uses to seek out his feathered finds.*

## Composition of Scent

As early as 1924, there were experiments regarding human scent by L. Lohner of the Physiological Institute of the University of Graz.  He noted his studies in a paper dated 1926 that involved "a female Doberman pinscher and blocks of wood which had been held by various individuals.  He said the dog could identify a block which had been touched by only one finger for a period of one or two seconds. Furthermore, the human odor was not masked when odorous substances such as bergamot, oil of cloves, or wild marjoram oil (when they) were applied to the test blocks. Trying to determine how long a block retained the hand scent, he found that it was lost faster in warm weather than in cold, and most slowly if the block was kept in a closed jar. It was not removed by soaking for two minutes in warm water, but could be eradicated by placing the block in a hot air dryer at about 150° C. for five to ten minutes or in boiling water for ten minutes."[6]

The CIA went on to say in the released documents that "*It is possible to draw several conclusions about the nature of human scent from these experiments and from other evidence.*

*First, the odorous substance must be somewhat volatile, since it could be removed by hot air. There are other considerations that support this conclusion. For instance, it is difficult to imagine how a dog could detect a person from a distance if the odorous material were not volatile. In one series of our own experiments, portions of trails were laid by rowing a boat along the shore of a lake, and it was found that a dog, trailing on shore, could determine which way his human quarry had gone without its having set foot on the ground. The shore line must therefore have been marked for him by vaporized scented matter.*
*Second, its volatility can nevertheless not be very high under ordinary conditions. Since it remains on sticks and clothing for a considerable length of time, it must have a fairly low vapor pressure.  Third, it must be rather persistent (in the chemical warfare sense), hence chemically stable and relatively dense with respect to air. Dogs can follow a*

---

[6] Human Scent and Its Detection.  Central Intelligence Agency Library.  CIA Historical Review Program.  Release in full, 22 September 1993. Updated August 4, 2011. CIA. McLean, VA. US.

*trail hours after it was laid, and their actions indicate that pockets of scent collect and persist in particular places under the proper conditions.*

Figure 17 K9 Ben. Handler: Sarah Platts.

*Fourth, since warm water did not remove the scent from Löhner's test blocks, it is not readily soluble in water. There is evidence that a dog can identify an individual by scent, although apparently with more than usual difficulty, even after a number of successive baths. Either it is very difficult to wash the scent off even with soap, or else it is replaced rapidly after a bath."*

In further follow up tests by the CIA, dogs could identify a stick which was handled by a specific human being when given a sniff of the hand of the individual. However, they could not identify the stick or individual when given a urine sample of the individual. They could identify the stick which was rubbed by solvents from human hair.[7] Interestingly humans could identify the scent of a specific individual part of the body that the scent originated (such as armpit, pubic, etc.) but could not identify which individual the scent came from. Additional information noted from these experiments concluded that[8]:

1. *Dogs appear to find some common individual scent produced by different parts of the human body, whereas to a human the different parts of the body have different odors. Urine, however, does not contain the individual's scent.*

2. *The substance of human scent, although not very soluble in water, is susceptible to fat solvents and can be extracted from hair by the use of these.*

3. *The characteristic scent does not change from day to day.*

According to the released document, human scent is comprised of[9]:

1. *Eccrine sweat probably has some odor, one which becomes more noticeable with bacterial decomposition.*

2. *There are apocrine sweat glands in all the hairier parts of the body (armpits, perimammillary regions, mid-line of the abdomen, pubic and anal regions) except on the head, where they are found only in the external ear canal and the nasal vestibule, not in the scalp or on the face. Apocrine sweat contains odorous materials, and the odor becomes more pronounced with bacterial decomposition; it is probably the main source of so-called "body odor." These glands do not*

---

[7] IBID.
[8] IBID.
[9] IBID.

*respond to temperature changes, but they are readily activated by mental stimuli. In animals, at least, they appear to be related to sexual attraction. Beyond that, not much is known as to why they exist.*

3. *Sebaceous glands secrete a fatty material that serves to lubricate and protect the skin which is called sebum. (These are found) over the entire body except for some parts of the feet, the palms of the hands, the palm sides of the fingers, and between the fingers. But sebum is found on all parts of the skin, including those where there are no glands, because it flows over the skin very rapidly. It is said to be very difficult to get even a small portion of the palm free from sebum, and it is estimated that it flows over wet skin at the rate of some 1.3 inches per second.*

It gets even more interesting when one considers, *"Thus it could be surmised that human scent, as a species, is the property of a major component (or set of components) characteristic of human sebum (say squalene), but that each individual has a unique mixture of various minor ingredients (say certain fatty acids or long-chain alcohols). Individual scent would be a blend, the major scent modified by various additives, like a series of different perfumes compounded on the same basic theme. Such chemical individuality is not without precedent, and it may even turn out to be the rule that the chemistry of living organisms displays individual variations around some central theme. In blood groupings, which have been studied rather extensively, it has been found that each individual appears to have his own characteristic pattern of blood types and sub-types, while genetically related individuals (racial groups) show characteristically similar patterns. It is possible, by determining the presence or absence of a comparatively few factors, not only to identify blood as human, but also to obtain information about the donor's genetic background and, potentially at least, to identify the individual."*

The CIA document goes on to note that[10]: *"Take a man standing in a field with a wind blowing across his body and a dog 100 yards down wind. Scent is transferred from the man's body to the air and is carried downwind to the dog. We will assume the man and dog have maintained their positions long enough that a continuous cloud of scent is present between them. As it goes down wind, the cross section of the cloud will grow larger and the concentration of the scent in the air smaller in rough proportion to the square of the distance. The concentration at any particular point will vary, however, not only with the rate of emanation of the scent, wind speed, and distance, but also with corrective factors expressing the effects of weather and terrain on the width and height*

---

[10] IBID.

19

*of the cloud, the earth's drag on the part of the cloud near the ground, and the tendency of the concentration to decrease with altitude."*

*"Having noted the apparent similarities in limited volatility, density, and persistence between human scent and chemical warfare agents, we shall adopt the values for these corrective factors that have been worked out for the travel of clouds of chemical warfare agents. Prentiss gives values for conditions which he lists as "favorable," "average," and "unfavorable" for a chemical gas attack. These conditions equally well describe good, average and poor working conditions for a dog."*

*"For the rate of transfer of the scent from man to air we can make an estimate on the following basis. Rothman estimates that an adult produces an average of at least 200 micrograms of sebum per minute.  We have noted that the sebum layer on the skin tends to maintain equilibrium, being replenished as fast as it is lost.  So we can use this average rate of sebum production to represent the average rate at which it is transferred to the air.  But presumably not all the many ingredients of sebum are odorous to the dog, and we shall therefore arbitrarily take ten percent of this rate, or 20 micrograms per minute (2 X10-2 mg/min) as the rate of transfer of the scent from man to air."*

*"Taking this expression as the rate of scent transfer, a distance of 100 yards, a wind speed of 6 miles per hour, and the values of corrective factors for "average" conditions, we get a concentration of scent available to the dog of approximately 10-12 milligrams per milliliter of air. For "favorable" conditions, using a wind speed of 2 mph, the concentration would be about 10-11 mg/ml, and for "unfavorable" conditions, with a wind speed of 12 mph, it would be about 10-13 mg/ml. It is possible, to judge from practical experience, that under "unfavorable" conditions 100 yards would be a little beyond the dog's effective range.  The spread between the concentrations available to the dog under favorable and under unfavorable conditions is about two orders of magnitude (10-11 to 10-13mg/ml).  Since scent concentration varies inversely with the square of the distance when everything else is constant, a variation in the distance by a factor of 10 would give this concentration change of two orders of magnitude.  It jibes well that a practical rule of thumb for the effective range of a sentry dog's detection by scent is 50 to 500 yards, depending on conditions, a minimum and maximum distance separated by our factor of 10."*

*"The concentration of scent available to the dog is exceedingly small. The value obtained for "average" conditions (10-12 mg/ml) represents only one millionth of a microgram of odorous material in a liter of air, a microgram being a millionth of a gram.*

*By weight, since a liter of air weighs somewhat over one gram, this means that the air 100 yards down wind contains one ten thousandth of a millionth of one percent of the odorous material."*

*"Although these results seem at first sight incredible, man in his own sense realm can also detect by smell exceedingly small amounts of odorous materials in air; and there are several substances which he can recognize in concentrations similar to those just calculated. Some minimum concentrations detectable by humans are the following:*

> *vanillin ............................................... 10-13mg/ml*
> *synthetic musk ................................... 10-12mg/ml*
> *mercaptan ......................................... 10-11mg/ml*
> *skatol................................................. 10-13mg/ml*

*In the light of these data, our fantastically small figures for the concentrations a dog can detect are not particularly unreasonable. It is only necessary to make the obvious postulate that some things which have little or no odor to a human must be quite odorous to a dog."*[11]

If all of this has your head swimming, fear not as we will present a simpler method to understand what is happening for the dog and handler. While scientists and chemists are able to duplicate human scent and cadaver scent in the laboratory, it is probably enough for us as handlers to know that scent is comprised of a myriad of factors and each human tends to smell differently to a dog, if the scent source is alive. Genetics, diet, medications, shampoos, hygiene, perfumes, etc. all influence the actual scent of the individual; in short, their lifestyle. The bacterial actions on the skin rafts we are shedding continuously have an impact on the scent itself. It can also be impacted by certain diseases and psychological conditions. Hence, all live humans have a distinctive odor; perhaps down to the DNA level. However, in death, we all smell alike. Learn as much as you can about scent and scenting conditions, and you will become a better dog handler.

## Basic Scent Theory

An Air Scent dog uses air scenting techniques to detect human odor. A Wilderness Air Scent (WAS) dog usually works in a woods or wilderness area but may work in other types of environments as well. The Air Scent dog searches the wind air

---

[11] IBID.

currents for human odor in an attempt to work a scent cone distribution to the primary source of the odor, the human being.

The Air Scent premise is demonstrated in the illustration with the smiley face signifying the scent source (which will be a person) and the triangle signifying the scent as it emanates from the scent source forming a scent cone if the wind direction was out of the west and blowing toward the east.

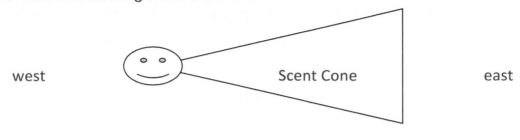

Figure 18 Scent Cone

(Note that scent can and will do many things other than form a perfectly organized scent cone as shown.)

Because of scent characteristics and response, the handler and helper need to be ever vigilant in setting up problems which place the dog in a position to pick up the scent cone...i.e. paying attention to the direction that the wind is blowing and placing the dog so that he will be able to have the scent blown into his face as shown below with the arrows indicating wind direction.

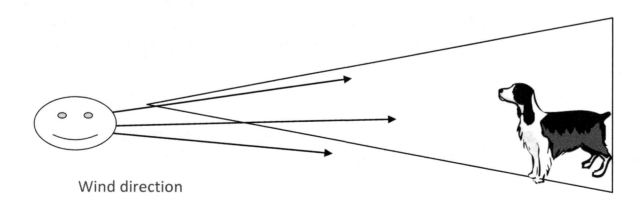

Wind direction

Some of the common characteristics of the scent picture include:

   • **Scent pools** which are formed in higher concentrations above and near the source of scent.  In this environment, the dog may need some assistance in identifying the strongest source of scent because scent is everywhere.  A handler could ask the dog to "check it here" and "check it here" gently moving the arm in a pattern to get the nose into each of the main areas of the environment.  In other cases, it will be up to the handler to pinpoint the source as the dog has told you that it is "everywhere" in this location.

   • **Scent cones** are formed when the wind moves the scent from the subject in the direction of the wind and if the dog is placed as the search cat is below...of course, not this close....he may not be able to detect any scent.

**Wind Direction**

**Scent Cone**

In the following illustration, the dog is most likely not in a position to pick up the scent of the person with wind blowing from east to west and the scent of the subject blowing away from the dog.  If the dog were west of the subject, this would be a good scent condition.

North

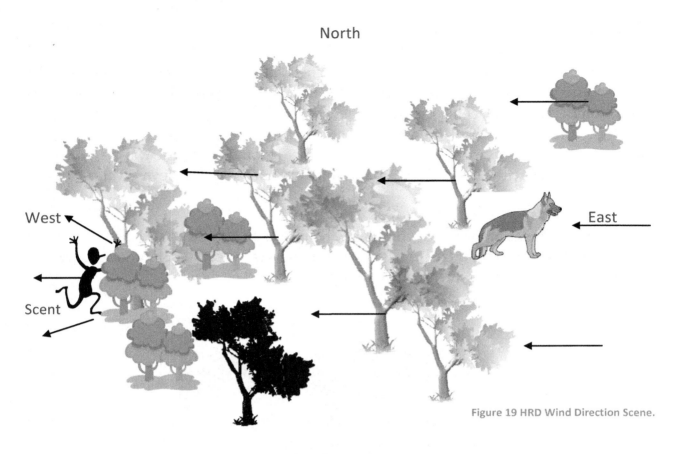

West

Scent

East

Figure 19 HRD Wind Direction Scene.

South

When setting up the search problem, it is critical to use the wind to your advantage as previously shown. This is how the dog is able to pick up the scent cone of the scent source and follow it to the location even when there may be other contributing scent factors.

Check the wind direction by using your eyes and looking to see which direction the leaves and brush are bending or leaning at the level of the dog's nose. You may also have a piece of surveyor's tape attached to your SAR pack or lead and be ever aware of the direction the wind is blowing. A puff bottle works well putting a puff of a small talc powder or chalky type powder into the wind at the level of the dog's nose...not near the dog. It does not provide as much information if you puff your talc six feet high in the air...remember where your dog is working. Although it is not always possible to work your dog in optimal wind placement, be ever vigilant in trying to do so.

● A **Scent Void** occurs when there is no scent discernible to the dog or may not be collecting in a particular location. This may occur when scent is rising straight up into the skies or simply lifted higher than the nose of the dog can detect.  It does not mean that there is no scent, but that the scent is not within the reach and detection of the dog at that moment.

## Factors Affecting Scent

Many factors may affect how scent travels.  Much of the information used today was gathered from firefighters who documented how fire travels, early experiments with federal agencies, and military information about chemical warfare.  Some of the factors which affect how scent will behave include:

## Temperature

- Scent will rise from the surface of the earth as the temperatures rise and drop to the ground as the temperatures decrease.    Most often it will rise in the morning and drop closer to the ground in the late afternoon as temperatures drop.  This is assuming there is a variation in the temperature of the area.  Sometimes it will even travel straight up, leaving little to no detectable scent for the dog to smell.

The following illustration might be described as **thermal lift with the primary scent rising straight up in warmer temperatures.**

## Environmental Factors

- Scent will catch on brush and other deterrents as well as move around barriers and buildings depending upon the wind currents.

- Scent may move across the valleys at the same height as the hill with the victim and collect on neighboring hills.

- It can create an **eddy** whereby it becomes a circular type of turbulence.

- **Scent pools** may form as scent collects on and around trees, buildings or other debris. It will certainly travel around any type of barriers, whether man-made or natural.

- Ground water can carry scent for long distances. Even underground waterways will carry scent away from the source and reappear in areas quite some distance from the actual body.

- Scent also washes downhill and into ditches which may then carry it, via water, further down the drainage or ditch with the body actually located beside or out of the ditch area.

## Structural Components and Barriers

• Scent can be carried through vents, openings in the woods line such as animal trails, or drop to the ground around a lone tree in a pasture. Handlers need to be aware that scent will "go around" buildings, lift inside elevator shafts, closed stairs, be distributed throughout the building when air conditioners or heaters are running, be lost through windows if windows are open, etc. Close windows and turn off air conditioning or heating systems when working inside a building. Allow the scent to 'settle' and then continue working the interior.

• Scent flows quite well through broken rubble, light framing or brick but goes around or is blocked by solid structures. It may also funnel through channels of debris or into and out of openings in the woods line (like game trails) or clear cut areas. When perplexed, stop your search and look around at the elements which may be affecting the scent and work your dog accordingly. Most of all one should be aware of the direction and strength of wind currents in the environment.

## Unusual Patterns of Scent

• Scent can do unpredictable things in certain situations. It is ever changing depending upon the environment. Situations such as higher wind gusts or turbulence can create very difficult if not impossible scent conditions for the dog. This can also occur with vehicular travel as cars drive by or emissions by the fire truck with the air conditioning running right next to the search area. Kindly ask them to move the vehicle or cut off the motor to avoid contaminating the search area further. Sun, wind, humidity and other outside influences can alter the scent picture varying as each hour passes.

• Scent conditions will be even more complex in a disaster situation with structural components layered on top of the person. This is another area requiring special training and experience before responding with your search dog. Buildings which pancake or collapse present many more challenges to the dog in order to pinpoint the location of the person. Handlers need to remember that these structural barriers can place scent in areas other than the location of the person.

• Basically scent conditions may be stable, neutral or unstable depending upon the influx of other conditions on the area; both natural and man-made. Handlers can practice identifying what the scent is doing in the search area by using surveyor's tape, puff bottles of powder, or similar aids. Remember to place the aid near the area where the dog will be working...not at "your" eye level. Then work your dog accordingly trying to place him in an optimum scent condition.  Remember that he is the scent locator, not the victim locator.

Additional quirks of scent movement include the following:

## The Chimney Effect

In a phenomenon called the "chimney effect" it can drop down around a lone tree in the middle of a pasture, and just as quickly go right back up that tree and be gone.  I recall one search for a missing man when in the middle of an open pasture/field area, my dog alerted at the base of the tree.  It was quite obvious that the person was not sitting under the tree.  So I got down on my hands and knees and sniffed the ground.  Sure enough I could smell the scent of cadaver.

I walked my dog out of the area for about five minutes and returned to the tree.  This time the dog did not alert or have any interest in the base of the tree.  I once again got down on my knees and sniffed…no scent of anything.  To be sure that I was not "losing it," I also asked the police chief who was accompanying me to sniff each time and he confirmed the same "sniff test" that I had experienced.   It can lift, drop back to the ground, lift again, and repeat this in a looping pattern.

The source of the scent…about ¼ mile away, a deceased subject who had been dead for about eight days.  Clearly, once the victim was located, and I returned to the same tree, it was upwind of the victim, slightly elevated from the location of the body which was on the edge of a wooded area.  He had crawled into a bush in a fetal position and died.   Could I have figured out the location of the body by this one experience…probably not.  Did it make sense later?  Yes.  Was it based upon laboratory evidence and research, nah….just plain ole common sense and experience.

This type of effect is also what baffles a handler from time to time.  One dog in the area alerting and ten minutes later a second dog walks past with no interest or indication of any scent in the area.  Was the first dog wrong?  Do we understand everything there is about scent?  No and nope.

● This is also sometimes called the "looping effect."

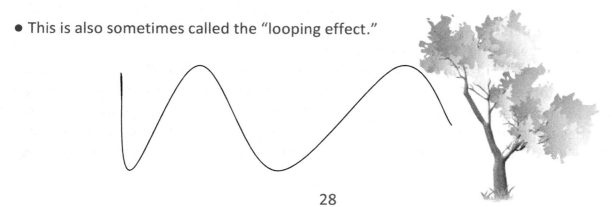

28

## Poor or No Scent Conditions

• Rain and humidity can enhance or destroy scent depending upon the amount of water and humidity. When there is no scent in the search area, scent tends to remain near the victim.

However, there can still be scent even after torrential rains. In one search, a murder victim was found with quite a bloody bath occurring. He was dragged from his car and shot multiple times and recovered within 12 hours. The location where his body laid was about six feet from a drainage ditch. The team was initially called in to assist in locating shell casings from the gun and/or a murder weapon. With permission, the dog handlers also worked their dogs on the area where the crime occurred. None of the human remains detection dogs has any problems alerting on the ground where the murder occurred. The following days, nine days in a row to be exact, torrential rains covered the area. On the 10th day, several of the dog handlers returned to the same area to see if the dogs could or would alert on the same crime scene. They showed mild interest in the location of the murder/body and went on to alert at the base of the drainage where presumably the scent has washed during the preceding days of rain. Even after a tremendous amount of rain, the scent of his blood remained to a threshold that the dogs were able to alert.

• There may also be a *scent void* if the scenting conditions are placing most of the scent above the level of the dog's nose. There may be no scent if conditions are so cold that there is no bacterial action on the scent as in extreme below freezing conditions. But again, depending upon the exact conditions, one never knows exactly what the dog can do.  In a drowning, three days into the disappearance on a lake, in freezing temperatures (32 degrees Fahrenheit and below), dogs were able to pinpoint the location of the body.  This was in a lake five miles wide and seven miles long.  The nose knew.

Handlers need to learn to recognize the scent conditions in order to read the dogs' behavior and work through the condition to the victim.  Variable wind conditions will play havoc with the scent.  It is a pure wonder dogs even find a victim with all the possible scenarios and scenting conditions possible but they do.

It is literally impossible to duplicate all of these conditions during training, but as many as you can recognize, the better your chances are of accurately reading the dog.  Try to set off a few smoke bombs to observe the wind conditions and you will have a pretty good idea of what the present conditions are.  Beware of dry pine straw or other flammable materials when using the smoke bombs...past experience.

The best scenting conditions are usually in the early morning and late afternoon hours.  To better understand your dog's scenting abilities and performance, study scent theory through books and presentations on scent characteristics.  A good place to start is *Scent and Scenting Theory* by William Syrotuk.  Remember, "Dogs are scent detectors...not victim locators."  It is our job to put them in an optimum position to maximize the probability they will detect the scent of a human being.

## Notes:

Information from the Central Intelligence Agency was obtained from the following sources:

1 Löhner, L., Pflüger's Archiv für die Gesamte Physiologie des Menschen und die Tiere, 202, 25-45, (1924).

2 Löhner, L., Pflüger's Archiv für die Gesamte Physiologie des Menschen und die Tiere, 212. 84-94, (1926).

3 The information on skin secretions in this section is derived from Rothman, Stephan, Physiology and Biochemistry of the Skin (University of Chicago Press, 1954).

4 Kalmus, H., British Journal of Animal Behavior, 3, 25-31, (1955).

5 See footnote 3.

6 Prentiss, Augustin M., Chemicals in Warfare (McGraw-Hill, New York, 1937).

7 See footnote 3.

8 Moncrieff, The Chemical Senses (John Wiley and Sons, New York, 1946).

Figure 20 K9 Tigger.  Handler:  Kim Veldeer.

Figure 21 K9 Grace.  Handler:  Lisa Altman.

31

Figure 22 K9 Bonnie. 2014.

Dogs laugh with their tails.

# Chapter Three

# Selecting a SAR Dog,
# Basic Equipment and Travel Plans

## Objectives

*Be able to list some important characteristics to consider when selecting a SAR dog.*

*Be able to list the contents of a Day Pack and a 48-hour pack.*

*Recognize appropriate precautions and preparations to make when traveling in a vehicle, truck and plane.*

In the dog selection process, one needs to consider the innate scenting abilities of the dog as well as the temperament, health, drive, motivation, size, sex, breed, and many other characteristics. Some of the breeds listed in the top ten list do not work well off lead and would not make a primary air scenting candidate; although will make a terrific trailing candidate...usually worked on lead.

When selecting a dog for SAR, enlist the assistance of other SAR personnel and experienced dog handlers who will help you locate an appropriate SAR candidate for your lifestyle and family. A handler with an apartment may not choose to enlist a bloodhound into the fold. A family with small children, planning to keep the dog inside the home all the time, may not chose a larger and more dominant breed. Research the breeds and select the dog which is right for you and your family. Select a dog that is appropriate for air scenting, works well off lead, and ranks in the sporting, herding, working or hound groups. These usually make good SAR dogs, if chosen with care, and handled with specific goals in mind using recognized training techniques. There are many other breeds which make good SAR dogs including border collies, Spanish Water dogs, and others.  Do not necessarily limit yourself to the common breeds.

Figure 23 K9 Tigger.  Handler: Kim Veldheer.  Socialization.

In addition, all search and rescue dogs should be solid in temperament and health. The handler will put a tremendous amount of time and effort into training the dog and should be able to use the dog in a working capacity until at least eight years old...often up to ten years old depending upon the breed and health.

Recognizing that health is the primary factor facilitating retirement at any age, it is wise to select a dog which comes from a responsible and respected breeder who completes the appropriate health testing on the parents, and if appropriate, the puppies. It is well and good to rescue dogs, and many become super stars in the SAR world, but others may get washed (removed from the SAR training program) due to poor temperaments or health issues, wasting valuable time and energy. These rescued dogs may make wonderful pets, but may not be such a great SAR prospect. Nothing is ever guaranteed.

Start with the best prospect you can afford. Know the characteristics of the breed you have chosen, talk with others living and working that breed, and what health issues are common in this breed. Is this a breed known for poor hips? Seizures? Thyroid issues? Vision deterioration in old age? Bloating? Or any of a host of other health issues which could affect the working life of a dog. Starting with the best does not guarantee a full working life but it sure ups the odds that your dog will be healthier for a longer period of time.

Explore all of your options, with the guidance of an experienced handler. I repeat...with the guidance of an experienced SAR dog handler. There is no magic formula, but many cautions when selecting a dog; rely on your mentor and choose carefully. While you are waiting on your chosen SAR puppy to whelp (after you have carefully chosen a reputable breeder) consider enlisting the assistance of the breeder in implementing some of the recent stress exercises with the puppies, as early as three days old. Some of these new techniques such as holding the puppy with the head down for three seconds, holding the puppy on his back for three seconds, placing the puppy on a cool towel for three seconds, removing the puppy from the rest of the litter for one minute, and similar exercises which are designed to slightly stress the puppy; theoretically developing certain chemical reactions in the body which will likely respond to stressors later in life with a more experienced or calm demeanor. These exercises are done for three weeks beginning at three days old. Of course a program of this type is more detailed than we shall cover and more scientifically based than we infer. In addition, be sure the puppy is socialized properly and exposed to climbing materials and various environments as appropriate. We shall cover more of this information in the Pre-School Basic Training chapter. Do your homework and implement, with your chosen breeder, whatever techniques you deem may help your puppy develop into a great working dog from day one.

## Equipment

Many times searchers are asked to search in areas that are near their vehicles, easily accessible by road and expected to take 4 or less hours to search. In those cases, an abbreviated day pack is sometimes used instead of taking the full 40 lb. pack into the woods with you. This assumes that you will have access to your gear and equipment within a short period of time, there are accessible roads within about five miles (which you could hike easily), and additional items are not anticipated or that would hinder your search abilities may be left in your vehicle.

However, if you are expected to go into areas where there is no easy accessibility to main roads, possible changing weather, possible extended search periods (such as 12 hours or overnight), hazardous areas (mountains, swamps, etc.) which may require additional gear, etc., a full Search and Rescue Technician II pack is recommended.

**Day Pack:** A day pack should be tailored to the type of search, the environment, seasonal needs (like insulated boots, etc.), and have support facilities nearby, if needed. It is usually considered the minimum equipment and supplies needed to search in the area which typically encompasses your primary callout area. Even though you prepare a day pack in a fanny pack or smaller backpack, searchers are encouraged to have a full 48-hour pack in your vehicle with all the supplies you may need for a full 48-hour deployment with no outside support, shelter or food. The decision to use a day pack vs. a 48-hour pack should be based upon proximity to support equipment, nearest road, etc.

A typical day pack might include:

WATER!!!                          Flagging Tape
Bug Spray/Cream                   Sunscreen
Lip Balm                          Duct Tape
Flashlight/headlamp               Batteries
Navigation Compass                Tape measure
Grid Reader                       Pad and Pencils
Knife-multipurpose and sharp      Large Leaf Bags Headgear/cap
Gloves

First Aide:
Band-Aids 6 – 1 inch              Band-Aid: large, knee, 4 inch
Aspirin, Chewable, 10             Ibuprofen, 10
Antibiotic                        Benadryl tabs
Roll of gauze

Emergency Blanket                 Boots
Radio - can be inexpensive family channel or TEAM issued radio
Bandana                           Tally beads
Matches                           Whistle

| Mole skin | Rubber Bands for Tracking Stick (not required of K9 handlers; flankers should have a tracking stick.) |

**Optional:**

| Extra compass | GPS |
| Additional flashlight with batteries | Food/snacks |
| Toilet paper | Rope |
| Towelettes | Carabineers |
| Extra socks | Rain gear |

## 48 - Hour Pack

A 48-Hour pack would include everything needed to pass the Search and Rescue Technician examination. Refer to your Fundamentals of Search and Rescue class for more information on the contents. It will expand the items to include:

## SAR Tech II Pack List

### Personal First Aid and Survival

| *4 acetaminophen or aspirin tablets* | *l plastic bag, zip lock, quart size for kit* |
| *4 antacid tablets* | *2 quarter for a phone call* |
| *2 antiseptic cleansing pads* | *l razor blade, single edge, safety type* |
| *l antiseptic ointment* | *l roller gauze bandage* |
| *6 band aids, various sizes* | *2 safety pins, large* |
| *l candle, long burning* | *l splinter forceps, tweezers* |
| *2 cotton swabs, non sterile* | *l space type blanket or space type sleeping bag* |
| *l duct tape ( 5-10 feet)* | *l whistle* |
| *l large leaf bag* | *l towelette, clean* |
| *8 matches in a waterproof container* | *1 moleskin* |

### Personal SAR Equipment

| *4 bags, various sizes, zip lock type* | *l pack, 1800 cubic inch minimum* |
| *l bandanna, handkerchief* | *l pad and pencil* |

| | |
|---|---|
| l cap or other headgear | 2 prussic slings (suitable for 9mm to 11 mm rope) |
| 2 carabineers (locking) | l rainwear, durable |
| l clothes bag, waterproof | l SAR personal identification |
| l clothing, adequate for climate | l shelter material, 8 X 10 plastic or coated nylon |
| l clothing extra set, suitable for climate | l scissors, multi-purpose |
| l compass, orienteering | l socks, extra pair |
| l flagging tape, roll | l sunscreen lotion |
| l flashlight or lantern | 1 tissue papers or baby wipes |
| l flashlight extra, extra batteries and bulb | 1 tracking stick minimum of 42 " |
| l footwear, sturdy, adequate for climate | 1 watch |
| l gloves, durable, even in summer | 2 water containers, at least liter size |
| l goggles, or eye protection, clear | l webbing, l" tubular-length suitable for harness |
| l insect repellent | 1 wire, 5-10 feet, woven steel |
| l knife, multi-purpose | 8 wire ties, plastic, self locking |
| l lip balm, with sunscreen | l mirror, small |
| l measuring device, l8 inch minimum | l metal cup or pot |
| l nylon twine, or small rope, 50 feet | |

## Optional Equipment

| | |
|---|---|
| 2 antihistamine, 25 mg benedryl | l rain cover, pack |
| 2 extra leaf bags | l sterno or stove |
| l extra water container | l sun glasses, 97% UV protection |
| l foam pad | l trail snacks |
| 2 food, nonperishable | l water purification tabs |
| Gaiters | |

In addition, the following is required by the FEMA handlers:

**FEMA Recommended Personal Equipment LIST**

| | | | | |
|---|---|---|---|---|
| Duffle | 6 shirts | 3 BDU blouses | 3 BDU pants | 1 heavy shirt |
| 1 ball cap | 1 light jacket | 1 heavy jacket | gloves/cold weather | gloves/hot weather |

| | | | |
|---|---|---|---|
| Rain gear | 7 underwear | 7 socks | 1 boots |
| 1 sneakers | 1 helmet with strap | eye protection | hearing protection |
| 1 bath towel | 1 wash cloth | hygiene/grooming kit | |
| Picture ID | eye glasses | sun glasses | ICS forms |
| 2 weeks of medications | flashlight/batteries/bulbs | | $300 cash |
| credit card | watch | Sleeping bag | |
| food/water for 24 hours | | | |

Figure 24 K9 Faith.  Handler:  Mike Holmberg.

39

Figure 25 K9 Tigger.  Handler:  Kim Veldheer.

## K9 Supplies

In addition, you will want to consider what supplies you will need when you have a dog with you.  At the minimum you will need:

Collar

Leash, (several)

PFD (if dog is working around water)

Crate (to transport dog in vehicle)

Soft crate (to take into motel room)

Dog food and treats

Toy rewards

Shabrack or vest

K9 First Aide Kit

Muzzle (if injured)

Towels

Crate mat

Pick Up plastic bags for clean-up

Paper towels

Regular dog shampoo and Dawn detergent (for decontamination baths)

Grooming tools (brush, scissors to cut out burrs, etc.)

Water for dog (plus bowl for car and at rest times, and whatever method you water your dog in the woods.  This could be sharing your bottle or hydration pack.)

Photograph and identifying criteria of your dog including Microchip number.

Immunization record of your dog showing up-to-date rabies shot.  (Note that some states require rabies every three years and other states every year.  If you are searching in a state that requires it annually, you need to be sure to keep that up to date, even if you reside in a state which requires it every three years.)

In addition, there are items which are considered comfort items such as the "cool mats." Think about what you will need and have it with you at all times...during training and searching.

## Suiting Up for the Mission

Figure 26 Goat Bell.

The **collar** should be a break-away collar (plastic buckle type...not the belt type).  This allows the dog to escape and break the collar open if it becomes caught on any brush, rebar, or other environmental hazard.  Many handlers prefer to add a small goat or turkey bell to the collar of the dog.  Most collars will contain identifiable information, name of dog, phone number, etc. to identify the dog as a search dog.  This helps the handler to listen for changes in the behavior of the dog when he is out of sight of the handler.

A lower pitched bell seems to conduct the sound better through the woods vs. a high pitched Christmas type jingle bell. A slower bell sound in the woods may indicate

that the dog is slowing down or has interest in something in the field. A faster bell may indicate that the dog has, for some reason, often when they get into the scent cone, increased his speed. No sound may indicate that the dog has stopped, ranged beyond the possible hearing distance of the handler, or lost his bell.

Figure 27 Shabrack or K9 Vest.

**Shabracks** or K9 vests are commonly used by search dogs. However, many handlers prefer to work their dogs naked (without vests) for several reasons. While a vest may make a dog more approachable to a lost person, if the person has drug connections or using drugs, it may be intimidating leading that person to believe that it is a drug search dog. However, in cases when the person may be afraid of all dogs, the vest may lessen the perceived danger.

Vests come in a variety of colors, designs and fittings. The vest shown in the photo is referred to as a bikini vest. It is cut to fit snugly against the dog's body. This is a better fit for wilderness work and helps the dog to avoid getting caught on vines or branches. Vests can also help identify working dogs during peak hunting seasons and provide an extra layer of safety. Vests increase visibility in the woods, especially for the average black or brown dog that blends into the environment. Therefore, each handler must decide for himself, based upon the mission and environment, whether they will chose to *suit up* in a vest or go bare.

In addition, the handler will develop a routine which will be a trigger for the dog that we are about to have some fun! That includes wearing your team shirt, appropriate long pants such as BDU's, appropriate shoes such as snake boots, and sporting your 'day pack,' which should include the necessary items you will need for the terrain to include first aide items, whistle, compass, etc.[12] the dog knows when you are suiting up...and

---

[12] Day Pack. A day pack includes deemed necessary items which may be needed in the field for the particular mission and terrain. Always take your day pack or a full 48-hour pack which will allow you to survive in the wilderness for up to 48 hours. See the appendix for sample day pack items.

looks forward to you *suiting them up* to go along. That is when the search collar with the bell comes into play. The dog knows.

## Traveling with Dogs in Privately Owned Vehicles and Trucks

Most often, you will be traveling with your dog in your own privately owned vehicle. The dog should travel in a wire crate, securely fastened to the car with seatbelts or positioning. This is the safe way in case of accidents or other unforeseen incidents. It is also a safe and comfortable place for your dog to rest in between missions, while you are being briefed, or not able to have him with you. Soft crates (made of fabric) are not advisable as dogs can and do chew out of them. They are, however, nice to bring into the fire department or motel room once you have settled down for the night. It is not recommended to put a dog in a soft crate anywhere and leave him unattended. He may be out and chewing on the comforter or destroying the room in his haste to try to find you but most convenient and lightweight when you are in the room with him. Another tip for the motel...take a sleeping bag into the room along with an extra large sheet to cover the bed. Do not allow your dog to jump up on the bed without first covering it to avoid leaving dog hair on the comforters and pillows. Sleeping in your own sleeping bag, even in the motel room, helps to ensure leaving the room cleaner. It is also a welcome addition to the cots in the fire department if that is where you end up spending the night. My pillow. My sleeping bag.

Dogs should be taught to go to the bathroom on command, one of the pre-school activities so that when you stop for gas, the dog will "go." Teach them a word which means, "go now." I use the word, "hurry up." This ensures a smooth drive, regardless of the distance. Dogs should also be willing to spend long periods of time quietly in their crates. They should also be able to remain in their crates for long periods of time while others (dogs and people) walk by. No one likes a barking dog.

Be prepared to load onto the back of a truck along with other dogs. You may be asked to leave your personal vehicle in one location and join others via the truck in a more remote location. You may have to load yourself, your pack, and your dog on the truck, handling all items yourself. Never let your dog go nose to nose with another strange dog (or other dog for that matter.) Keep a shorter lead on him and teach him to ignore other dogs and handlers. Practice makes perfect.

# Air Travel

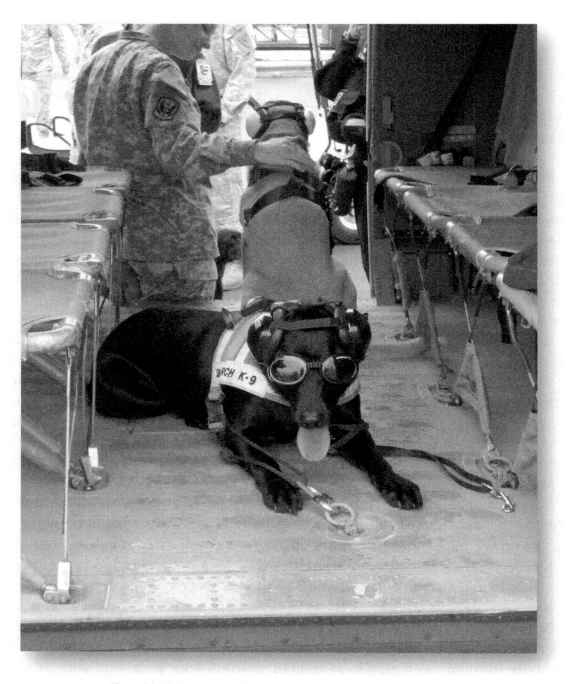

Figure 28 K9 Cirque.  Handler:  Craig Veldheer.  Helicopoter Operations.

Air travel may involve transporting your dog either in the cabin of the plane or in the cargo hold of the plane. As these requirements are ever changing and vary with each airline company, you should check ahead of time for the requirements and be prepared to show a current (within 14 days) health certificate signed by your veterinarian, the latest immunization records, present with a search vest on the dog, and be in your SAR uniform. Some airlines will not accept dogs, period, so be sure to check prior to arrival and confirming travel plans.

It is helpful to allow the dogs to "train" on a plane also...i.e. load and unload on a hot and cold helicopter (hot referring to engine running and cold referring to no engine running.) Contact your local civil air patrol to enlist their assistance in allowing your dog to load, fly a short distance, and land. Ask for loading, flying and unloading instructions before approaching the plane or helicopter. There are protocols for this including always approaching from the front of the plane. But never approach without instruction and permission from the pilot.

In any case, think through the demands of traveling with a dog and practice by taking your dog out of town for a night. You will realize what you need the most and develop a deeper bond with your K9 partner. Nothing says love like sleeping together.

**Dogs teach us many things about being a better person that people don't teach.**

Figure 29 K9 Bonnie. 2014.

## Out of Town and Out of Country Deployment Requests

From time to time, if you have worked in this field long enough, you will receive a request to assist in a missing person case which is across the nation, or out of the country. These requests need to be considered with full forethought and planning. By no means should you accept an out-of-country deployment unless you have pre-planned for this. It is easy for the family to request your services. It is not so easy to get your dog to the location, obtain maps, security, lodging and subsistence, cooperation of the local law enforcement, and get your dog BACK to the United States. Unless this is an official request from the reigning law enforcement agency of the country, or specifically endorsed by the proper authorities in your home country, politely decline the request and offer to try to find some in-country assistance for the authorities. Never set out to assist (with the best intentions we are sure) without clearing your presence and the intended search area with the local law enforcement authorities. Yes, the family wanted me to search the yard of the suspected murderer...did they share that little piece of information with me? Nah....just wanted some help searching for their daughter. Whew, dodged that bullet...barely.

If the request is legitimate (i.e. by the appropriate legal authority, consider the following information when deploying out of the area or out of country. Regardless of the requestor, never accept a deployment into conditions for which you are not trained or experienced. It never quite works out as well as you would hope.

## Preparing to Deploy Out of Country

Out of country deployment requires a series of immunizations and a passport as well as appropriate current health certificates for your dog; usually no more than two weeks old.

## Out of Country Immunizations for the Searcher/Handler

1. Tetnus-Diptheria (The latest dosages have whooping cough in them also...and everyone 50 or above should have one of these). FREE At some Health Depts. Check your state for availability.

2. Measles Mumps, and Rubella: Free at some Health Depts. (Two doses are available) —one month apart.

3. Malaria (need a prescription from your doctor...these are pills); (Individuals may be asked to take one per week beginning two weeks before the scheduled date of departure, one per week during the trip, and one per week for eight weeks following return to the US.)

4. Typhoid (Should call the local Health Dept and make an appt to get this immunization).

5. Polio - Free at some Health Depts.

6. Yellow Fever (Should call the Health Dept to make an appt to get this immunization).

7. Hepatitis A and B (this is a series of shots).

8. Rabies (painful)…if needed.

Check with your local health department or physician for recommendations based upon where you may be going to search and the type of conditions.

## Personal Medications (check with your medical doctor for personal recommendations.)

- Broad Spectrum Antiobiotic: request Rx from your physician.
Ask for a broad spectrum antibiotic like Cipro to take care of diarrheas that are caused by bacteria. Regular Immodium won't take care of bacteria caused diarrhea.

- Immodium – regular stress diarrhea.

- Ibuprofen – swelling and pain.

- Tylenol – fever.

- Aspirin – for dogs.

- Tums – upset stomach and also for dogs.

- Benedryl – swelling, insect stings, allergies.

- Tylenol – pm – sleep aid.

- Nausea meds: like over the counter Nauzene.

• Any prescription medications which you regularly take.

Figure 30 K9 Cirque. Handler: Craig Veldheer.

Figure 31 K9 T. C. Handler: Pam Bennett.

48

# K9 Preparations

1. General Physical well-being exam at your regular vet.

2. Up to date Rabies immunization. (I prefer a booster if the last shot was over a year ago); bring copy of rabies certificate with you. Signed with an original signature by the vet.

3. Parvovirus Booster.

4. Bordetella Vaccination.

5. Lepto Vaccine. Leptospirosis is common in stagnant pools of water and is spread through the urine of infected animals- especially RATS, which are likely to be even more numerous in a disaster.

6. Preventic Collar: prevents ticks (which carry so many diseases); Put on the day prior to Deployment. Cut to size back at home and do not leave the excess collar on the collar in case the dog wants to chew on it...poisonous. Lasts three months.

7. Advantix, single dose application to the neck for fleas, mosquitos, ticks. *By Bayer* is Labeled to repel fleas, ticks and mosquitoes.

8. Neo Predef powder: for cuts, scrapes, dog and person.

9. Doxycycline: Begin dosing the day of deployment and continue throughout the entire deployment. This takes care of many tummy issues, etc.

10. Metronidazole: for diarrhea caused by bacteria.

11. Mometamax: Ear drops for an ear infection.

12. Microchip K9: Take with you the chip number and documentation.

13. Ivemectin: Administer ½ cc. once per week for worms. OR other worm meds as prescribed for your dog by YOUR vet. This will take care of everything but tape worms. If you end up with tapes, see your vet for Drontal.

14. Tums to help prevent stomach upset.

Check with your local vet for additional recommendations for your specific dog. Label all medications and the purpose of each.

## K9 Supplies and Gear

K9 Food for the duration of the deployment.
Long lead.
Six foot lead.
K9 Vest (for flight).
Collar and spare collar.
Collar for night work like lighted collar (if conditions allow working in a collar).
Dawn detergent for decontamination if needed.
Soft Crate. Or Airline Crate if flying in cargo.
Treats or reward item.
Brush, comb, scissors, flea comb.
Waste bags for poo pickup.

## Documents to Bring

| | |
|---|---|
| Passport | Copy of Birth Certificate |
| Copy of Social Security Card | Drivers License |
| Credit Card | Immunization Card |
| K9 Rabies Certificate | K9 Immunizations Card |
| K9 Microchip Documentation | K9 Health Certificate |

Be sure to check with each individual country to be sure that your dog will not be kept in the country for quarantine for an extended period of time before allowed to enter or leave the country.

## SAR Supplies & Gear

Standard First Aid Supplies.
NASAR SAR Tech Pack (make sure you have extra batteries, bulbs, etc.)-See list attached.

Ear protection, Eye Protection, Knee Pads, Hydration Pack, Helmet w/ Chin strap
Extra empty garbage bags

## Personal Supplies & Gear

Water purification pills
Protein/energy bars
Boots, Knee Pads, gloves, rain gear, walking shoes, hat
BDU's, t-shirts (long and short sleeve)
Lightweight jacket
Heavyweight jacket
BDU shirt or vest
Day pack – Waist Pack
Personal and grooming supplies
      (brush, comb, toothbrush, toothpaste, soap, shampoo, conditioner,
      deodorant, etc.)
Something to sleep in when in groups/crowds (like sweat plans, shorts and a t-
      shirt,   etc.)
Socks, underwear for daily change
Picture ID
Towel, Wash clothe
Dirty Clothes Bag
Eye glasses (spare glasses), sunglasses


## Misc.

Luggage Tags
Cameras, disposable
$300 cash
Watch
Food & Water for 24 hours
Spiral Notebook, pens, pencils

Trading Cards, business cards, etc.
Radio, pager, cell phone
Credit Card
Sleeping Bag
Basic ICS Forms for Assignments and Briefing


## Pre-Preparation Coursework and Information

NASAR SAR Tech Certification or Equivalent
First Aide & CPR Certification
Hazardous Materials Awareness

51

ICS (Incident Command Systems) 100, 200, 700, 800 (additionally work on 300, 400)
MLPI (Managing the Lost Person Incident)
Advanced Search and Rescue
Technical Rescue Classes (such as ropes, confined space, etc.)
Helicopter Operations
USAR & TF Awareness (Urban Search and Rescue and Task Force)

Figure 32 K9 Grace.  Handler:  Lisa Altman.

Figure 33 K9 Ayla.  Handler:  Pam Bennett.

Figure 34 K9 Carlos climbing a ladder.  Handler:  Shelley Wood.

# Chapter Four

# Pre-School and Basic Training

### Objectives

*Recognize the value and skills needed by the dog prior to beginning SAR training.*

*List skills in basic obedience and agility which help to prepare the SAR dog for training.*

*Understand the importance of proper socialization of the SAR dog.*

---

Why in the world would a person want to teach a dog to climb a ladder? Or slide down a slide? Or go slow or fast? Or right or left? Under and over? And just about every other obedience and agility feat one can imagine. The search dog that is "schooled" in basic obedience, agility and sociability with other people and dogs is the perfect candidate for SAR training. He is better prepared for the eventuality of logs and downed trees in the woods, and crossing a ditch with water, riding in the back of a truck with other SAR dogs, able to climb up on a house destroyed by a tornado, comfortable with unsteady surfaces, and generally able to confidently face any obstacle he may face in the course of a search mission. The dog that can take direction with hand signals (when loud noises are all around him), does not spook when there is gunfire or sirens, and who comes when you call him is a joy to train in SAR. Step-by-step, list the skills you may encounter and begin to expose the dog to small increments of those skills until he (and you) are at ease in those scenarios.

*The photograph on the preceding page shows a piece of equipment used to teach a dog to climb a ladder. It is a bit easier when the ladder is initially backed by plywood as shown in the photograph. Encourage the dog to take one step at a time with high quality treats. Later, remove the plywood from the ladder.*

Figure 35 K9 Tigger. Handler: Kim Veldheer.

## Pre-School and Basic Training

Basic socialization and physical conditioning are critical to prepare a dog for search dog training. This topic has been adequately covered in *Building a Basic Foundation for Search and Rescue Dog Training,* written by this author. Community dog training classes may also be helpful to teach many of these skills. Some of the recommended skills are:

1. *Basic Obedience commands* such as come, sit, down, up, stay, back, easy, and leave it.

2. *Basic Agility commands* such as over, through, in, up, down, right, left, turn, climb, and slow.

3. *Basic commands* such as watch me, wait, stop, and go.

4. *Search commands* such as check-it, find, search, etc.

5. *Socialization* such as good behavior around other dogs, and people of various races, ages, health conditions, and mental status.

6. *Traveling skills make life easier and more pleasant when the dog can behave,* such as riding in the back of a truck with other handlers and dogs (each on lead and with a handler), riding quietly in a crate in a car, loading into a truck or other vehicle, riding on a four wheeler all-terrain vehicle, and waiting quietly in the vehicle with the tail gate open while other people and dogs walk by. No one likes a barking dog in a crate that just will not stop.

7. Loading onto a helicopter, or any other type of vehicle including a myriad of boat types is important if you ever plan to be transported or work off of another type of vehicle.

8. *Terrain maneuvers should be practiced...* such as crossing a shallow stream or ditch, crossing over a log, jumping up into an abandoned building, entering a crawl space, climbing a hill/mountain/rubble pile, following a drainage or ditch, and traversing all types of environments such as fields, agricultural plantings (corn fields, etc.); especially terrain features which are common to the area where the dog might search.

Climbing a ladder...

...and what goes up

must come down.

Figure 36 K9 Carlos. Handler: Shelley Wood.

57

Figure 37 K9 Gypsy learns to climb a ladder.  Handler:  Christy Judah.

Figure 38 K9 Hope, Handler:  Chris Holmberg.  Note Victim behind dog in rubble.

In other words, the dog should be taught and exposed to any type of surface, scene or situation which he may encounter during training or a search, including the sounds of sirens and heavy machinery.  Temper the activity or exposure to the age and ability level of the dog and handler.  Do not encourage stressful physical skills which may harm bone development and growth such as jumping up or down from vehicles or other raised props prior to age one because the bones are still developing.  Most skills can be taught using lower, age appropriate heights such as putting a board on two cinder blocks which will mimic a catwalk and teaching beginner agility skills.  All of these skills make the SAR dog safer and more controllable in uncontrollable circumstances and terrain. When the dog has adequately completed these types of preparatory activities, he may be ready to officially begin his SAR dog training.  It does not mean that he has mastered all of the above, but is regularly exposed to these training scenarios in addition to his SAR training.  Together they create a well-conditioned dog ready to confidently approach a search.

## Teaching the Check it Command

Handlers should teach the dog the "check it" command, which in essence means for the dog to put his nose and sniff where or in the direction that the handler is pointing. This can be done by making a large sweep with the arm and the finger pointing in a particular direction, inside a bush, or general location. At that location, very close to where the finger is pointing, there will be a food treat...just a snippet of something like a piece of hotdog. Once the dog goes into the correct place, say, "good check it." Repeat as needed, slowly phasing out the hot dog bits but still praising the dog with a "good check it" each time he does what you are asking, and treat with the hot dog snippet from your hand. Phase out the hot dog by having a hot dog in 50% of the locations, then 30% of the locations, and eventually none of the locations. However, when there is no hot dog in the location, the dog will still be praised by the handler for having checked it and get a reward from the handler. Eventually there will be "koli[13]" or the live person at the check it location and a treat or reward will be forthcoming upon each *find. This may be used later in a cross-trained dog...and not something that is critical to concentrate on at this point.*

Figure 39 K9 Beau. Handler: Nancy Jacoy.

---

[13] Koli is an Indian word for spirit and sometimes used as a command word when searching for human remains. For instance, the handler may say, "find koli."

# Preparatory Training

Dogs need a minimum level of obedience, agility and general socialization prior to entering search training.  This is not to the extent that a kennel club might require for obedience or agility titles, but a level of control so the handler will know that the dog will respond to basic environmental stressors and commands which will keep the dog safe and allow the handler to place the dog in the area desired for searching.  You will want to have a solid recall or 'come' command.  These skills should be trained prior to entering the next phase...directed searching, alerts/indications, and refinds.  In addition, these skills should be a part of the regular training regime.  You may want to consider beginning each SAR dog training exercise with ten minutes of obedience/agility/general skill training to set the tone for the day.  It will continually reinforce the needed obedience and deter lazy responses in the future.  Many a SAR dog has trained their handler to accept less than the original trained behavior by slowly eroding the behavior into an *almost did it* behavior.  It is less work to keep up the requirements than to have to re-train Fido after he has so adeptly eroded the original behavior and taught you to accept a different or modified behavior.  Continually reinforce what you expect in the field.

## General Training Tips

It cannot be emphasized enough that each step along the training process, including the preparatory training, will be forever ongoing.  Each phase should be solid before moving to the next phase.  Handlers have long known that if you move too quickly into the next step, it will only come back to bite you and you will be 'fixing' things which do not work in the field over the long run.  Therefore, practice each step until you feel confident the dog understands it, performs it to a high degree of reliability, and it is rote before moving to the next step.  If all else fails, and you find yourself with a broken chain of skills, or unable to complete the task as described, return to an earlier step for several weeks and then progress through the steps again.

Handlers are encouraged to return to the basics from time to time for K9 motivation.  This means to back up to the early stages with fun, quick and motivational exercises.  Training will be on-going for the life of the service dog.  You should also document all training and searches in whatever format you choose.  When *you* become lazy, either in training or maintaining your paperwork (logs), it is difficult to regain the motivation and self-discipline to return to regular training and documentation.  There is no quick and easy way to avoid putting in the work, time, energy, and dedication into search work.  All components must be present or you are moving backwards.   Stay positive, stay informed of the latest practices, attend workshops and seminars as available and possible, and align yourself with a reputable team to share the training and search experiences.  These components, not your ego or other political purposes, will lay the groundwork for a successful career.

---

Figure 40 K9 Lauren with puppy Bonnie.  Handler:  Christy Judah.

Figure 41 K9 Brynn.  Handler:  Tracy Spilsbury.  Ready Position.

# Chapter Five

# Reward Systems, Alerts and Commands

## Objectives

*Describe the benefits of a toy or a food reward.*

*Be able to demonstrate a suitable ready position for the search dog and handler.*

*Understand the differences between the victim-focused vs. a handler-focused search dog.*

*Define an alert, an indication and a final response behavior.*

*Recognize a passive and an aggressive final response behavior.*

---

The training in this manual incorporates an "alert" or "indication" by the dog; meaning a trained behavior to indicate to the handler that the dog has indeed found the missing person. An alert[14] is defined as a characteristic change of behavior in the dog in response to an odor such as a live or deceased person and recognized as such by the handler. The "components of the alert may include change of behavior (COB), alert, interest, and final response or indication." [15]

---

[14] Alert: a characteristic change in ongoing behavior in response to a trained odor as interpreted by the handler. SWGDOG.    http://swgdog.fiu.edu/approved-guidelines/sc1_terminology_abcdefghijk.pdf
[15] Components of an Alert: SWGDOG.
http://swgdog.fiu.edu/approved-guidelines/sc1_terminology_abcdefghijk.pdf

## Types of Rewards:  Toy or Food

SAR dog trainers generally propose either a toy or a food reward system to imprint and motivate the dog.  Depending upon the training techniques used (like whether or not a recall/refind will be used), using a toy reward may not be convenient and interrupt the progression of steps thus interrupting the training process.  Many handlers prefer to use food rewards for the smaller steps and the toy reward for the final response once the victim has been located and the dog has taken the handler back to the victim during the recall/refind.  And ……. *No* …… praise is not good enough.  Every step will include praise but praise alone will not take you through an eight hour search and more advanced training.  Do not make the mistake of thinking that your dog will continue to work for only praise in the long run.

Figure 42 K9 Lauren with Nose in Rubble. Handler: Christy Judah.

Examples of toy rewards might include using a stick, cloth Frisbee, tug toy, or other soft item easily put into the handler's pocket or attached via a tether to the uniform of the handler.   (Be aware that some dogs will try to self reward; so if a stick

66

throw is selected as the toy reward, be prepared for the dog to self reward when tired or stressed with any available stick in the area. Another down side to a stick reward is that others can easily pick up and throw sticks quite unintentionally which may distract the dog. Think about a boat scene with the dog in the boat. A diver on the boat picks up a stick to throw out of the boat...and out goes the dog trying to walk on water. (And yes, this has happened.) The toy reward used should be reserved for training purposes only and be a high drive toy easily taken into the field but so interesting to the dog that he will do anything for that toy or game. It will be used only during SAR trainings and searches.

Food rewards might include canned sausage, hot dogs, chicken bits, steak bits, or other soft foods easily eaten (select a treat which does not take a long time to chew so as not to interrupt the process but for a few seconds). The food choices for a food reward must only be used during training and must be of such a high quality that the dog is focused on the handler knowing that the treat is coming shortly. The food reward may also be used with a *marker* (which may be a word like "yes" or a special sound or a standard clicker) indicating that the exact behavior preformed at that moment is the correct one and a reward is coming very shortly. The reward must come quickly and not be delayed or the purpose of using a *marker* before the actual reward is lost in the process. Timing is everything in training and especially when using a *marker*.

Figure 43 K9 Charlie leaving the missing subject and returning to the handler in a recall/refind. Handler: Jim Ware.

The preferred choice of reward is based upon the dog...not the handler. It should be the thing which holds the focus of the dog and works for that particular dog (breed or individual). Even prior to beginning SAR dog training, the handler can identify what the most likely reward will be and have that available at every training session *and* search.

Note: Praise is part of the reward system but is not the only aspect of reward. Remember, the dog is doing this for the reward after the game...and a chintzy reward is not worth much after a six-hour search or training session. Select either a toy or food reward or a combination of both to set the stage for a more successful training session and continued high working drive.

## Selecting a Search Command

Select a word which you will use each and every time you begin the wilderness air scent exercise or search. Examples of commands might be "find," "search," or something cryptic like a German or Dutch term. Whatever you choose, use the same word each and every time. This will be your command to begin searching. For the purpose of this book, we shall use the term, "find."

## The Ready Position

It is helpful to select a 'ready' position to begin any search command or exercise. An example of a ready position is holding the collar of the dog with the dog positioned between your legs, head facing forward and withers about even with the knees. Handler is bending down slightly holding the collar and gently talking to the dog to rev up the motivation with words such as, "are you ready...want to go find someone?" The purpose is to focus the dog, act out a regular routine which in turn tells your dog that we are about to go search.

Other ready positions might be, dog on right side, facing forward, handler holding collar until the beginning command is given, handler kneeling beside dog, handler behind dog, etc. Choose a position that is comfortable for you and the size of dog you have. In the ready position, the lead should not be attached. Now you are ready.

Figure 44 K9 Beau.  Handler:  Wendy Long.  Ready Position.

# Focus Based Systems:  Victim Focus or Handler Focus

SAR dog trainers have long had divisive conversations on whether the SAR dog should be trained to be most focused on the handler or the missing person…as some would say whether they are *loyal* to the missing subject or to the handler.  This refers to whether the dog will remain with the missing person (once located) and this is the person who rewards the dog (i.e. giving the food to the dog or providing the toy for the dog) or whether the dog will leave the missing person once he has found him and return to the handler with a heightened focus on getting a reward from the handler; or whether the dog goes to the victim but is more focused on the handler than the victim for his next command or reward.

This book proposes that whether you train for victim or handler focus or *loyalty* depends upon the type of training, environment, and the discipline being trained.  If the dog is trained for disaster response to find missing persons in a rubble pile, the accepted training techniques for a dog team such as the Federal Emergency Response Team (FEMA) require the dog to remain with the missing person (or the strongest scent of the person) and bark for a continued length of time.  In this case, the handler is tasked with hearing the dog alert/bark and move towards the dog.  This type of training involves victim focus since he remains with the missing person instead of doing a recall/refind.  It is appropriate in this scenario and safer for the dog to remain with the strongest scent rather than traverse the rubble pile back to the handler and take the handler to the victim.

In wilderness air scent, a well-developed recall/refind system places the handler notification (returning to the handler, alerting with a trained behavior and taking the handler back to the missing person) as very efficient.  In that environment, a victim focus stance (whereby the dog remains with the victim) requires the handler to now find the dog.  When dogs work in very close proximity to the handler, this may not be a problem.  For dogs which work in extremely large search areas and out of sight of the handler most of the time, the refind and focus on the handler may be more efficient, achieve the ultimate goal of finding the missing person in short order and allow the handler to more effectively cover the search area (rather than following the dog so closely so they can see the dog.  Another down side to the handler working so closely to the dog in this type of search is that many handlers tend to then "follow" the dog instead of covering their area.  In a technique involving a re-find, the handler is not required to "keep up" with the dog.  Instead the handler and their team cover the search area in a particular pattern while the dog surveys the environment from many angles trying to pick up the scent cone.  Once the dog has picked up the scent and indicated such to the handler, the handler leaves their pattern searching to follow the dog to the victim.

In a victim focus situation, the dog may or may not do a trained recall/refind and remains with the victim until the handler arrives.  In reality, in a wilderness search, the dog may be quite some distance from the handler when he finds the victim, and without a recall/refind it will be up to the handler to "find the dog" once the dog finds the victim if the dog stays with the victim instead of returning to the handler.  The distance may also be too great to hear a sustained bark alert; therefore a handler focus approach seems to work very well in those types of environments.  Keep in mind that in some environments where the visibility is large and wide, a handler focus or refind may not even be needed...after all you can see the dog for a great distance...no problem.  Handlers need to decide what works best for them.

In a recent conversation with the special operations canine unit trainer from a branch of the military, the term *focus* is used rather than loyalty when discussing these ideas.  When explaining our *loyalty* terminology, they quickly made the connection with their use of the word "focus."  Even in bomb detection work, they train their dogs to maintain handler loyalty at all times so they can continue working toward the "next bomb."  This is not to say that they want their dog to leave a bomb location until given the command, but the primary 'focus' is on the handler and the handler commands and rewards.  The reward is not coming from the bomb.  Since few rewards come from cadavers or even a live find, it seems a bit silly to this author to always pretend that the reward is coming from the HRD sample, although in the beginning training the reward (if food) is given in close proximity to the HRD sample, to create a pleasant association with the HRD smell and the food reward.  However, it is out of the realm of this author to think that the "dog thinks" that the *reward is coming from the HRD sample itself.*  No, it is more of a let's let the reward smell a bit like the HRD sample.  (Others disagree and many trainers (especially law enforcement) choose to toss the ball or tug at the source material (in the human remains detection realm) so the dog stays focused on the source material.  This is a totally different type of training and will be discussed in more detail in a subsequent book on how to train the human remains detection dog.)

In the live find situations, it is a manner of the "party" at the end of the find and both the victim and the handler reward the dog and celebrate the find together.  In most cases, the handler is more exuberant and joyful than the victim.  Later training may have the victim or helper in a prone position, unconscious (acting), or fearful of the dog.  Do I want my dog to be *loyal* or have undying focus to this fearful person?  Or drunk?  Or drugged?

Some of the special operations trainers in the military are now teaching a *combat alert*.  In this type of training, the dog is taught to alert or indicate to the handler at a distance from the actual target person.  This is a safety technique that has been useful in providing a safety buffer zone for the dog and handler.  If the dog alerts 50 or even 100 feet away from the actual subject...the handler can now send in the armed personnel to apprehend or complete the find. This is an interesting variation on the presently used methods by volunteer organizations who seem to stress the dog be in very near proximity to the subject. Even in normal searches, if there are such things, it seems prudent to allow or even teach the dog to alert/indicate in the near proximity, but not necessarily directly beside the subject. Again, a drunk subject, drugged, or just plain fearful subject (not to mention a mentally handicapped or psychologically disturbed person) may indeed harm the dog. Hence, this author is not exceptionally keen on requiring the dog to make contact with or be in the *touch vicinity* of the subject if the dog chooses not to do so. Not necessary. Just some fodder for thought.

In another situation the progression of wilderness air scent live find might involve the dog finding the victim and doing an initial recall/refind but only once...placing victim focus above returning to the handler multiple times (even if that is needed more than once due to distance and pace of the handler).

Once the dog and handler are both at the victim location, a victim focused approach involves only the victim rewarding the dog with no or little involvement by the handler. During initial training, I propose that the victim and the dog handler both reward the dog. This provides a positive 360 environment with all participants showing an involvement in the reward, even flankers or others present. There is no doubt about the behavior of the dog...he did it right and everyone has now acknowledged it.

I have to share a situation at a seminar once when my handler-focused dog was encouraged to be more loyal or focused on the victim and I was told to step back, twenty feet away, and allow only the victim to food reward the dog. The dog had found the victim, done a beautiful recall/refind, took me to the victim and looked to me for the reward just as we had trained. This time I stepped back and looked away while the victim gave the dog his treat...a high quality food reward and praised the dog. The dog literally walked away from both of us and went off to explore the surrounding woods...with what appeared to me as a perplexed response.

In an immediate follow-up exercise the dog refused to even search when given the search command. I cried all the way home that afternoon thinking I had totally destroyed the groundwork I had already completed with my dog and ruined a perfectly good SAR dog. She rode on my lap all the way home (instead of the crate) with me praying that I could undo what I had just done. Luckily, two days later, while training our usual handler-reward technique, the dog again responded to me in his normal fashion. He was happily receiving his rewards from me, the handler, the victim, and any other person present. Lesson learned: *if it ain't broke, don't try to fix it.* So if your training is successful with one system...use it. The handler focused reward system works for me.

The handler-focused approach has been my preferred method of training for wilderness air scent and human remains detection primarily for the safety of the dog. We are looking for many types of missing persons and some are dangerous and/or armed. I am not concerned that the dog is sitting one foot from the missing person or that the dog even wants to be that close to the missing person. Dogs have a sense of what is safe and what is not...and I believe that in many cases they can determine whether it is safe to go "in" to the victim versus near the victim. However the handler needs to be aware of the possibility that the dog may begin to take short cuts and become lazy about going in to the victim and decide to alert and wait on that reward before actually finding the victim...but while in scent. This becomes a problem to be corrected by being sure that the victim is in fact at least partially involved in the reward system and the handler knows where the victim is and whether the dog has in fact been "in" to the victim before rewarding. Do not allow sloppy work.

Figure 45 K9 Charlie takes the handler back to the missing person during a refind. Handler: Jim Ware.

73

Figure 46 K9 Faith on rubble.  Handler:  Mike Holmberg.

I once had a dog which was certified to do therapy work.  We visited local schools and annually did a program for the entire 5th grade, one or two classes at a time.  In between classes, the dog came into my office, and rested quietly at my feet under my desk.  Word spread quickly when I brought the dog to school and the children flocked to my office to see and pet the dog in between classes.  He tolerated hundreds (literally) of little hands that petted his ears and head and lovingly felt his soft fur with little more than a nod of his head; until one group of kids came into the office. This group approached him in the same way as the students earlier, gently approaching him and reaching for him one at a time. He let out a low growl and made it clear as he looked at me that he did not want these kids to come near him. After several years of doing this program I had never observed him respond in this manner. I softly intervened and asked the kids to let him rest as we had a class in a few minutes and he was a little tired. They retreated and we completed our programs with no further incident or similar responses. What could have happened to cause the dog to respond in a different manner when these particular children came into the office?

The three boys were classified as Exceptional Children and labeled as having Behavioral Disorders. Although each situation was different, they had all had previous violent episodes, were difficult to control at times, and took various psychotropic medications. According to my observations they had behaved no differently than any other child among hundreds that day but the dog responded differently to these boys. Although this is an anecdotal story, it brings to mind the insight that this dog had into something different about these kids... their DNA, their psyche, the scent of the medications...something different triggered the dog reaction. Regardless of what it was that the dog sensed, the important note is that the dog sensed something different and responded differently. (It is of note that there are research studies documenting a variety of pheromones which are produced by schizophrenic individuals that are identifiable. It is quite natural to assume that dogs can detect these. In 2012, there were research studies in Sweden regarding dogs detecting insect pheromones.[16] In these studies dogs were able to identify trees with certain insects presumably based upon the pheromones the insects produced.)

This *school experience* caused me to consider the dangers of searching for strangers. Regardless of the amount of information available to the handler, many unknown aspects can be interjected into the scene. Is the person an alcoholic? Is there a possibility of known or unknown mental illness? What medications might affect the person and his scent? Is the victim suicidal? Does the victim have a weapon? Is the person afraid of dogs? Is there some other reason why the dog need not approach the victim too closely or expect that the victim is going to be the source of his reward—each and every time? Too many unknowns are interjected into each search and for the safety of the dog, I prefer that the dog be loyal and primarily focused on me and my search crew, recognizing that good things can and do come from the missing person but not to the extent that the dog does not look to me for his security, safety and primary reward.

---

[16] Kelley, Pat. Dogs Detecting Insect Pheromones. Fumigants and Pheromones. Issue 105. Winter 2013.

Have I been accused of anthropomorphizing[17] my dog?  Sure I have.  But my methods have worked, my dogs have had finds, and my training experiences have helped to shape other SAR dogs who have also have successful careers.  It works for me.  It has worked for them.  So do many other training techniques.

In the case of human remains detection, the reward does not come from the missing person/victim…who is now deceased.  Unless you trick the dog into thinking that the reward is coming from the victim during training (which will not be the case during the actual search) it seems to be a mute point encouraging victim loyalty/focus.   There is no live victim to reward the dog.  In addition, the environment may be such that the handler needs to quickly take the dog out of the immediate area to preserve the crime scene and/or remove the dog from the vicinity for hazardous reasons.

Certainly, no handler wants the dog to touch, mouth, or have any other interaction with a deceased body.  I would much rather see the dog look to me for the reward.  Handlers do need to be cognizant of an unintentional audience such as possible family members, media, or other spectators (which especially might be the case in drowned cases, etc.).

In addition, if the dog is cross-trained, and you have used victim-focus in one type of search and handler focus in another type of search, it may complicate the training process and confuse the dog.  Therefore, the handler should consider choosing either handler or victim focus based upon the type of search he expects to respond to most often and training technique he plans to employ.  This book will primarily use a handler focus.

Figure 47 K9 Deva hunting.
Handler: Linda Murphy.

---

[17] an·thro·po·mor·phize:  Show Spelled [an-thruh-puh-mawr-fahyz] Show IPA verb (used with object), **verb** (used without object), an·thro·po·mor·phized, an·thro·po·mor·phiz·ing. to ascribe human form or attributes to (an animal, plant, material **object**, etc.).  Source: Dictionary.com

Figure 48 K9 Juno on Pause Box. Handler: Beckie Stanevich. Photo courtesy of Shelly Burton.

## Selecting an Alert/Indication /Final Response Behavior

*Alerting* or *indicating* is the trained behavior that the dog demonstrates when he has found the missing person. Most often the dog will find the missing person, return to the handler, demonstrate that alert behavior, and then upon command (usually 'show me') turn around and return to the missing subject. Note that the 'show me' command is not used when the handler is in close proximity to the victim or remains (in the case of deceased) but when the dog is some distance from the victim in a re-find situation. More will be explained as we progress, but understand that when the handler and dog are in very close proximity to the remains or the live person and the handler keeps telling the dog to "show me"...they may in fact be playing the old children's game of *hot or cold...constantly asking the dog to show me until they actually get it.* In this case the dog may begin alerting every little spot and hoping to ultimately hit the jackpot reward if he keeps indicating on everything. Do not fall prey to this bad habit. This common mistake will be discussed in more detail later.

The alert behavior or *indication* is a term which is sometimes interchangeably used by various parts of the nation to mean the same thing....a change in behavior by the dog. However, the SWGDOG committee has suggested that an *indication* is the dogs' response to the odor in the manner in which it has been trained, independently and without distraction."[18]  An *alert* is a change in the ongoing behavior in response to a trained odor.[19]  These are very similar terms with subtle variances.  This is also sometimes called the *final response behavior*.

However, some individuals define them a bit differently with the indication being the initial change in behavior of the dog to a defined odor and the alert as the trained behavior the dog does to indicate to the handler that he has in fact found the target odor.  For purposes of this book, an *indication* shall mean that *trained* behavior the dog exhibits and is recognized by the handler to mean the dog has found the target odor.

Figure 49 K9 Beau alerts on a previous burial site with a sit alert.

Handler: Wendy Long.

The handler should observe the dog as training progresses to see if a natural behavior presents itself that could be tied to a command for search and rescue use.  For instance, if the dog has easily learned to sit, the handler may want to consider a sit as an indication behavior for the dog. In this instance, after the dog has found the victim and returned to the handler, and the dog will sit in front of the handler to indicate to the handler he has indeed found the missing subject.  The handler will then say, "show me," and the dog will turn around and return to the missing subject.

The steps to teach this behavior will be discussed in later chapters.

---

[18] Indication:  definition according to SWGDOG.
http://swgdog.fiu.edu/approved-guidelines/sc1_terminology_abcdefghijk.pdf.  P. 26.
[19] IBID.  P. 3.

# Passive and Aggressive Final Responses

The handler may select either a passive or aggressive final response. Examples of passive alerts include a sit, down, point, look back at handler or other behavior which does not involve an active involvement with the source of the odor. In an aggressive alert, the dog might bark, dig, scratch, bite, or any combination of the list. While years of teaching handlers that a passive alert is preferred over an aggressive alert for human remains detection which will obviously cause less disturbance to the remains, many would suggest that through experience one finds that well-trained dogs do not tend to destroy evidence in the field or injure the person; rather they have a natural tendency to recognize it as a deceased human and shy away from disturbing it. Not always, mind you, but in all cases that I have personally observed or have knowledge about. With this information, it becomes a mute point to demand a totally passive final response in all cases. With the amount of damage and disturbance that natural predators in the woods exhibit, a SAR dog is most likely not going to hinder the investigation, evidence or remains in any appreciable manner. However, handlers need to be aware of the dog and their personal treatment of the deceased and living and report any such disturbance to the law enforcement officials so they may note the change in the crime scene, if any.

In the world of search and rescue, biting is not allowed in wilderness air scent, nor is any aggressive interaction with the subject such as jumping on the victim; think 90 year old Alzheimer's patient or three-year old child. This could easily injure or scare the missing person.

Additional behaviors which might be used as an alert (when the dog lets the handler know that he has found the missing person in a wilderness air scent scene using a re-find) include jumping up on the chest or hips of the handler (not recommended for large dogs or small handlers), barking at the handler, taking a handkerchief from the handlers belt loop, or any of a myriad of behaviors which the dog does not normally do in the course of field work unless they have found the person.

A small and very minute behavior such as an ear twitch is not sufficient for this purpose. The behavior should be one that the handler can easily identify, describe to an evaluator or fellow crew member, and is reliable in communicating to the handler that the dog has found the person. It should be easily identified and recognized by anyone watching the dog work a problem. In addition, this is a behavior used only with the handler and the dog, not involving the victim in any way.

A dog 'alerting' on a victim by pawing the victim or any other behavior involving touching the victim is not necessary or desired. It is a different type of training based upon identifying a particular person using a scent article from a scene such as a police line-up. This is a type of training used by law enforcement in some situations to identify a perpetrator and seldom used by search and rescue volunteers to find a missing person, although it is not out of the possibility of incorporation into a search scenario. However, it will not be taught as a part of this curriculum. For now we will concentrate on the communication between the dog and the handler, independent of the missing person.

Remember, one is never quite sure what type of condition or frame of mind the missing person may have...drunk, drugged, psychotic, depressed, extremely surprised, happy, sad, old, fragile, frail, etc. We also do not know whether the missing person is armed with a weapon. It is best, in my opinion, to avoid contact with the missing subject in most cases and instead allow the dog to develop a routine and bond with the handler and not the victim. With this background, the handler can now proceed to implement the step-by-step process and train the dog.

---

*Happiness depends upon ourselves.*

*Aristotle* (384 BC – 322 BC)

Figure 50 K9 Beau at three months old doing a refind with handler Wendy Long following.

**Chapter Six**

# Step-by-Step Training

### Objectives

*Describe the steps involved in training an off lead
wilderness search and rescue dog to find a lost or missing person.*

*Describe the air scent technique
to teach the Re-find in a wilderness environment.*

*Be able to explain the basic steps involved in training
a wilderness air scent dog using a modified reverse chaining method.*

*Recognize successful training versus unsuccessful training
and be able to remediate or step back in training in order to move forward.*

---

The basis for wilderness air scent training involves ultimately teaching the dog to complete the following progression of behaviors for a non-scent specific dog[20], which incorporates a refind[21]:

1. The handler gives the "search" command and sends the dog out to search an assigned area.

---

[20] A non-scent specific dog is one which does not require a scent article and searches for any human being in the search area. The dog may locate multiple victims or searchers in adjoining search segments if within the scent cone or detection distances.

[21] Refind: a deliberate act of a dog to return to the handler after finding the source of scent; then return to the source of scent with the handler following him until they reach the source of scent.

2.  The dog leaves the handler, runs out in front or to the side of the handler 'searching' for the missing person.

3.  The dog finds the missing person, turns around, and returns to the handler.

4.  The dog indicates to the handler via a trained behavior (alert/indication) that he has indeed found the person and the handler recognizes the trained behavior.

5.  The handler commands the dog to "show me" meaning "take me to the missing person." (This assumes that the missing person is out of sight of the handler and the dog at this time.)

6.  The dog turns around and returns to the missing person with the handler following him.

7.  If necessary, the dog keeps returning to the handler, as the dog may be much quicker moving through the terrain than the handler, until they both reach the missing subject.

8.  The dog and handler arrive at the location of the missing person and the dog is rewarded.

There are trainers who will teach the dog to find the missing subject and remain with the subject. The handler must *then* find the dog and subject. This does not seem to be the most efficient method to work a dog in a wilderness environment when the vision of the handler is likely obstructed by terrain features, trees and brush. Even if the dog remains with the subject and begins to bark to guide the handler to the subject, this method does not seem, to this author, to be the most efficient in a wilderness environment. Therefore, the method of training where the dog stays with the victim is not described in this book.

However, a handler may adapt any of the suggestions contained therein to meet the needs of their area, training preferences and terrain. One certainly can recognize the value of training the dog to remain with the subject in a disaster scene where it may be unsafe for the dog to return to the handler on unsteady surfaces, and safer to just remain with the primary live scent source. This type of disaster training (on rubble) requires very specific training techniques and should not be employed by handlers who have not been exposed to and trained on rubble and disaster piles. This requires a different skill set...hazards, environment, and protocol. It completely different process than wilderness air scent. Do not be confused into thinking you can do the same on a rubble pile that you can do in a wilderness environment. You may injure yourself or your dog. But do realize that in this type of environment (rubble), regardless of what you train, IF your dog has been trained in a re-find, even though he is trained differently for rubble work, there is a real possibility that he will revert back to the refind when 'stressed.' Stressed can mean, out of his comfort zone as far as the rubble pile, noises, vibrations, shakiness of the footing, number of people present, or any other factor that he is not trained around on a regular basis. When stressed, he *can* and many times *will* revert back to his originally taught behaviors and alerts.

The progression of expected dog behaviors varies when there is no scent, no missing person, or no human remains in the search area. There are variations of the training based upon whether a refind is incorporated in the training or the dog is trained to remain with the scent source. The emphasis in this guide will be on including a refind in the exercise to find the scent source.

There is no *one* right or wrong way to train a dog and one must consider various terrain and search conditions. Exposure to various training techniques can help the handler decide what may work best with an individual dog and combining various techniques is permissible. Training and actual implementation on a search may vary from trainer to trainer, handler to handler, and dog to dog, based upon many factors. However, once a training regime is established, the handler must seriously consider the value of trying out different training techniques with the same dog or total confusion may result. When attending seminars, a good trainer will understand and adapt the exercise to the training techniques which you have been using if they have already proven successful with your dog. However, if you are not successful with the techniques you have been using, by all means, move on to something else. Experience will teach the handler how to adapt a training technique for the dog based upon previous training. Experience will also teach the handler to recognize a dog which needs to be washed from the training program due to health, lack of motivation or other factors. The same holds true when it is time to retire a tried and trusted partner.

---

"It is not rocket science," I was told at my initial training session many years ago. It seems to still appropriately describe the steps involved in training a search and rescue dog. However, many conditions may come into play during the process. The handler needs to be able to recognize and adjust for these ever changing conditions during the training exercises.

Many trainers will tell you that it is much harder to train the handler than the dog…given that the dog is gifted with the drive to work. Be that as it may, we shall concentrate on the system which will assume that:

A. The handler is mentally able and motivated to train a search and rescue dog and above all has agreed that "they do not know it all after 18 months or two years." Plenty of new handlers are eager and good students until they reach about 18 months into the program…and then with a few searches under their belt, a fancy uniform, a SAR dog vest, and tons of ego, they know more than the trainer, and set off on their own path to eventual destruction and failure. When their first dog retires or is injured, they are at a loss as to how to train the next dog, where to go for help, and end up floundering until they return to the fold, realize that this is a team effort, respect and respond positively to mentoring, accept suggestions by those who truly have the training, experience and wisdom. There will always be those out there who know more than you and have more experience. When you close those doors to personal growth in dog training and as a searcher, you become a liability and not an asset. Open the gates to welcome mentoring and advice from others more experienced than you, and you will one day earn respect and grow into the role of a mentor for the next generation. Revere your trainers…do not alienate them. By all means avoid burning the bridge…they are the ones who got you started, showed you the ropes, shared their knowledge, time and energy, and helped you develop as a handler.

B. The handler should have basic canine training skills which have been demonstrated in getting the dog to the current level of training which may include a sit, down, stay and basic agility skills such as teaching the dog to go 'over' an object, 'under' an object, and the like; and has adequately socialized the dog to allow for comfortable training with other handlers and dogs. Teams may want to consider encouraging and even requiring the handler to obtain a Canine Good Citizen certification with the American Kennel Club, a great introduction to documenting good doggie social skills.

C. The handler is willing to devote the time to train a SAR dog. This venture requires a huge commitment of time, energy, and funds to allow the handler and dog to travel (gas and lodging expenses, fees for seminars and workshops, etc.) It requires the time, energy, and commitment *with* the blessings of the handler's family and employers, to respond to searches at all hours of the day or night. It does little good to spend upwards to a year training a SAR dog only to be able to decline most searches due to family or work commitments. And showing up for an hour is not a lot of help…the job continues until the victim is found or the incident commander suspends the search. You are needed for an operational period (if at all possible) which usually lasts 12 hours. Plan to provide services for extended periods of time. That is usually what it takes unless it is a very specific human remains detection mission which may include only a very small area. This is not usually true for a live find mission; if it was, the law enforcement personnel would have already completed the chore.

D.  The handler needs to have a clear criminal record…none to be exact. Most law enforcement personnel are uncomfortable working side-by-side with felons…you just will not get asked to participate; and the handler needs a clean driving record…no speeding, DUI's, DWI's, etc. LEO remembers.

E.  The handler needs to be prepared to be a "searcher first" and a "handler" second. Obtain the required team training such as a CPR and First Aide certification, Search and Rescue Technician Certification (through the National Association of Search and Rescue), Hazmat (Hazardous materials) training, incident command training (ICS 100, 200, 700 800 minimum which are available on the FEMA website at www.fema.gov) Helicopter Operations, Crime Scene Preservation, Boat Operations, Four Wheeler Operations, etc.) Being a top-notch dog handler involves more than dog handling…it involves being the best searcher you can be and then having a trained K9 to assist in the process.

F.  Lastly, the handler needs to be able to recognize that not all searches end in a loving embrace with the missing person, smiles, and happy families. Sadly, many conclude with suicides, fatal accidents, homicides, and death scenes. Crime scenes can be most disturbing and beyond any fathomable preconception of what they will look like. Handlers need to recognize the emotional impact that this type of scene may inflict upon their own psyche and be prepared to welcome critical stress debriefing and counseling afterwards. Searchers need to remember that at all costs regardless of the outcome, the missing person is being returned to the family, a gift which will be forever cherished. The heart and the mind must be healthy to handle this type of work.

So, if all is well, you have checked off the above, the desire to train a search and rescue dog is burning in the heart, and you feel you have what it takes to be a good searcher and dog handler, let us begin by understanding the steps we expect of the search dog in a Wilderness Live find mission. It is not possible to know, every single time, whether the missing person is alive or deceased. Treat every search as a potential crime scene protecting all evidence and clues. (Refer to Chapter 8 for Crime Scene Protocols.)

During the process, we will be using what is sometimes referred to as back-chaining in the step-by-step training...or a loose version of back-chaining, since the steps we are considering are not exactly taught in reverse, but under the guise of a similar plan. In other words, we will be teaching the refind first, and then adding steps along the way to ultimately get to the desired sequence of events we would like to see in the dog.

Our initial training steps will vary a bit from step 1 consecutively and train the refind first. A helper is needed for the process, so recruit a neighbor, team member, or family member who can help you on a regular basis, if only for ten minutes a day but pretty consistently on a daily basis at first. Consistency is crucial in the process, so plan to train five days a week...whichever five days you choose, and additionally, work on the prep skills (obedience, agility, social skills, etc.) for a few minutes every single day. Remember that it should always be a fun time for both you and the dog. It is up to you to keep it fun and safe.

## Weather Considerations

Weather should not be a factor in your training schedule unless it becomes extreme...above 90 degrees or below 32 degrees. And of course, as you progress, you will train in all types of weather conditions to be able to judge the fitness and abilities of your dog to react to various weather conditions. You should never train or search in extremely dangerous situations such as hurricanes, tornados, etc. If the weather conditions put you or your dog in danger, decline the request. You should also consider what temperatures your dog is normally at rest...a dog kept in the air conditioning all the time will have more difficulty searching in warm to hot weather. However, a dog kept in a warm environment all the time may not have more difficulty searching in the cold temperatures, unless extreme. Use common sense and avoid setting your dog up for failure based upon *at rest conditions* and the breed. Certain breeds may tolerate specific temperatures better than others. Think about what is safe and works best for your environment, you and your dog.

Author note: At the end of each step in the training process is a brief section for the trainer to record personal notes...perhaps what worked well, what was accomplished, dates of training, or other notes. Maybe even a picture of your dog practicing this step. Good luck and happy training...remember it should be fun for you and the dog.

# Wilderness Air Scent Training Steps

## Step 1 - Runaways

a. The helper shall place the dog in a ready position holding onto the collar...no lead attached.

b. The handler will be facing the helper and dog and standing several feet in front of the dog waving a high quality treat and keeping the attention of the dog by talking to the dog "where am I going, watch me...watch me." The handler quickly leaves the dog and runs away about 30 feet still waving his arms and talking to the dog. There should be no barriers or distractions between the helper and the handler. Each individual faces the other in full view during the exercise. (Do not use any barriers or try to hide behind anything at this stage.)

c. The helper continues to hold on to the dog collar in the ready position while the handler excitedly runs away from the dog with a cheerful, happy voice, calling the dog, "Brownie, come." The handler should accentuate the 'come' command clearly. (The dog has already learned what the command "come" means in general obedience training outside of SAR practice.)

d. About two seconds after the handler says the "come" command, the helper turns loose of the dog. Sometimes the dog will be pulling against the helper as he continues to hold the dog until the handler gives the command.

e. The dog should run excitedly and directly toward the handler.

f. As soon as the dog arrives at the handler, the handler gives the food or toy reward praising the dog in a cheerful excited voice saying, "Good come." This reward continues for at least three minutes. Time the reward and you will see that many handlers cut the reward short, not giving the dog the full motion of a satisfying reward session. The dog will let you know when the reward is enough as they finish their food, stop playing with their toy, or walk away after a happy rub down party version of the game, "Good come." Remember... happy, happy, happy party at the end for whatever length of time the dog desires...up to about five minutes. Some want more, some less.

Notes: Some men do not tend to get quite as excited and happy acting as many women and should make a concerted effort to get excited so that excitement transfers to the dog and in turn motivates the dog. It is ok to be a little goofy and use a higher pitched voice at this time; no one is looking and the more excited and happy you are the happier and more excited your dog will be. Motivating the dog and enjoying the exercise is the key to a successful exercise.

Repeat this exercise four or five times each time originating the dog at the helper. The dog should quite naturally go to his owner/handler. If by some chance the dog becomes distracted by something in the periphery of the environment, try to remove that distraction and try again. If the dog shows no interest in returning to the handler, you will have to figure out why the distraction is more enticing than the dog running to the handler. Possible reasons could be:

--wildlife such as birds or squirrels or other animal scents are overpowering,

--toys in the area are more alluring,

--the reward is not of a high enough quality to entice the dog to come to the handler,

--the dog does not have a solid "come" command,

--noise in the area is distracting the dog, or

--other people or dogs in the area are interfering with the exercise.

If you can isolate why the dog is not choosing to participate in the exercise, try to work on that independent of the search exercise. In other words, if the dog is crittering (following other animal tracks, scent or the animal), teach the "leave it" command, work the dog on a long lead (20 feet) initially and give a strong correction each time the dog begins to follow a critter scent. Teaching the *leave it* command works well for food or poisons found in the wild (gasoline, paints, etc.) or frozen chicken on a rubble pile after a tornado (as everyone in the world seems to have frozen chicken in their freezer and it is sure to show up in your search area.) Once you have taught the "leave it" command, try the SAR exercise again...another day, another location.

If the initial area is too distracting, find another location which is safe, fenced if you have one available, and free of distractions. Note that in some cases, without the "come" command, it is about impossible to continue. This foundation work must be reliable and accurate to proceed. It will only set the handler and dog up for failure down the road if you cannot complete step 1 in a timely and correct fashion. Get the foundation work done before moving to step 2.

If the reward is not a high enough quality, find a higher quality reward which will hold the attention of the dog. If you must go to the toy reward, do so and try the exercise again. Some dogs much prefer a toy reward and it can also be combined with a food reward in future steps. So at this point, try the exercise again but reward with the favorite toy which is ONLY used during SAR training. Once you have this exercise reliable, proceed to step 2. And for all future exercises, be *sure* you have the toy with you.

**Frequency:** Repeat this exercise 4-5 times in a row before stopping. Always end the exercise on a positive note with the dog being successful. Do this for 6 days in a row, preferably twice a day for a total of 24 – 30 repetitions.

**Definition of Success:** The dog happily runs from the helper to the handler in a fairly direct path, readily accepts the reward, and is excited to receive praise from the handler.

If you have difficulty completing Step 1…consider taking a week break and try again from the beginning. If after a few tries working through the process of Step 1 you dog does not "get it," consider having a trainer evaluate your dog and your handling skills to determine if you or the dog is the problem. They may see something that you do not recognize or be able to evaluate your dog and help you determine that this dog may not be a good SAR candidate. In any case, do not proceed with Step 2 unless you have mastered the simplicity of Step 1. It is no shame to "wash out" a dog from the SAR program and find another one who has an interest, ability, and desire to learn the games. Some dogs clearly do not buy into this process and will never make a good SAR prospect regardless of the dedication or skill of the handler. It is best to realize that if there is not some gain in the training process over the course of a month, you may want to consider other options. If the dog proceeds successfully, happily move to Step 2.

Personal Notes:

_____
_____
_____
_____

# Step 2: The Show Me Command

a. Begin the exercise the same way as step 1...the helper holds the dog. The helper releases the dog and the dog runs directly to the handler. However, this time, the *come command* is eliminated and the handler just excitedly waves the food reward in front of the dog as he runs away, perhaps saying "watch me," to keep the dog attention. The helper says nothing as he releases the dog.

b. As soon as the dog reaches the handler he (the handler) quickly says "show me" and begins running back toward the helper in a direct path. The dog should follow or lead the handler back to the helper. The handler should be aware of how critical the timing is as they say, "show me" and begin to run toward the helper. This should be immediate with no lag between the arrival of the dog and the command to "show me." Timing is crucial to rewarding the desired behavior. If you have a lag time, you are rewarding lagging around before returning to the subject/helper.

c. As soon as the handler and dog arrive at the helper, the dog is rewarded by both the handler and the helper and they have a party....three to five minutes. The party includes lots of praise directed at the dog, happy voices, cheerful talking to the dog, food and/or toy offered. The party does not deteriorate with the helper and the handler discussing the exercise and what took place. There is time for that *after the party is over*.

Notes: If the food reward is in place, the dog gets food tidbits from both the handler and the helper. If the toy reward is in place, the handler provides the toy for the dog and allows the dog to play with the toy in whatever fashion is most rewarding for the dog. This could either be running around with the toy (prize) in his mouth or bringing the toy back to the handler for a game of fetch. (If a tug with a toy is employed, be sure that you are not inadvertently teaching the dog to be aggressive. Check with your local dog trainer or a more experienced trainer to be sure you are not creating a problem. I do not recommend tug but others very positively and successfully use this method of reward. Make an informed decision and implement in a positive manner if you use a tug.)

**Frequency:** Repeat this exercise 4-5 times in a row before stopping. Always end the exercise on a positive note with the dog being successful. Do this for 6 days in a row, preferably twice a day for a total of 24 – 30 repetitions.

**Definition of Success:** The dog leaves the helper, runs directly to the handler. The handler says, "Show me," and the dog immediately turns around and runs back to the helper with the handler running behind the dog until he reaches the helper. The dog understands the sequence of events and begins to immediately turn around and return to the helper running in front of the handler.

Personal Notes:

_____
_____
_____
_____
_____
_____
_____
_____
_____
_____
_____
_____
_____
_____
_____
_____
_____
_____
_____
_____
_____
_____
_____
_____
_____

# Step 3: The Formal Refind

In step 3, there is a change in the sequence of events. The progression will be the same; however, at this step the handler starts the exercise by holding the dog in the ready position instead of the helper. We will now have a formal 'runaway' and incorporate the refind.

a. Handler holds the dog by the collar (no leash) in the ready position. Handler gives the search command... "FIND." The dog takes off to run to the helper on a direct path. (The helper can be calling the dog's name and trying to keep the attention on the dog.)

b. Once the dog reaches the helper, the handler begins to call the dog back to him if the dog does not immediately turn around and start running back to the handler. The dog returns to the handler.

c. The handler immediately gives the "show me" command as the dog reaches him, and immediately the handler begins to run toward the helper. The dog follows or leads the handler toward the helper. The dog will learn quickly that once he reaches the handler, the path leads directly back to the helper for the *final party*.

The handler may give a very quick, small food reward when he initially returns to the handler but it should be a quick reward (only if needed) before heading back toward the helper for the final party. If the dog comes back to the handler and immediately turns back to return to the helper, no reward is needed. If it is given in the early stages of training, it will be extinguished later on by slowly eliminating this reward. Extinguishable rewards are eliminated by only rewarding periodically, such as rewarding 2 out of 3 times, then 1 out of 2 times, then no reward at that stage of the exercise.)

d. Immediately upon arriving back at the helper (the refind), the party begins and the dog is rewarded for 3 to 5 minutes as the dog desires.

**Frequency:** Repeat this exercise 4-5 times in a row before ending the training session. Always end the exercise on a positive note with the dog being successful. Do this for 6 days in a row, preferably twice a day for a total of 24 – 30 repetitions.

**Definition of Success:**   The dog reliably leaves the handler when given the "find" command and runs to the helper.   The dog turns around in short order (within 45 seconds or less) and returns to the handler.   The handler tells the dog to "show me" and the dog immediately turns back around and returns to the helper.   This is done with 100% reliability.   (It is done correctly 10 times out of 10 exercises.)

Personal Notes:

_____
_____
_____
_____
_____
_____
_____
_____
_____
_____
_____
_____
_____
_____
_____
_____
_____
_____
_____
_____
_____
_____
_____
_____
_____
_____
_____
_____

# Step 4: Incorporating the Indication

At this stage of the game, the dog will be asked to perform a trained behavior, an indication, to let the handler know he has found the helper. This is a behavior which was previously trained, apart from the SAR exercises and may be a sit, down, bark, or any other behavior put to a command. As the dog returns to the handler after first finding the helper, the handler will *prompt the indication by commanding the dog to do it* before giving the *show me* command. In other words,

   a.   The dog is released to find the helper with the *search command*.
   b.   The dog finds the helper and returns to the handler.
   c.   The handler tells the dog to perform the indication behavior (sit, up, down, or whatever will be consistently used.)
   d.   The dog performs that behavior.
   e.   The handler gives the "*show me*" command.
   f.   The handler and the dog go running toward the helper and arrive at the helper.
   g.   The final party is held.

This stage should be continued until the dog learns to perform the indication without a prompt. Do not sit back after a few repetitions and wait to see if the dog will perform the indication. This just teaches the dog to take his sweet time performing the indication. Prompt the indication behavior until the dog actually returns to the handler and immediately does the behavior without prompting. If the dog does not immediately do the behavior, prompt until he does.

Remember, when selecting the initial indication behavior, it is easier to select a behavior which the dog does naturally, so during the previous stages, watch for a possible behavior. If the dog naturally sits when he returns to you, consider selecting that as an indication.

**Frequency:** Repeat this exercise until the dog understands and repeatedly performs the indication behavior upon return to the handler without prompting. Always end the exercise on a positive note with the dog being successful, even if you have to prompt that indication. Do this for 6 days in a row, preferably twice a day for a total of 24 – 30 repetitions.

**Definition of Success:** The dog reliably performs the indication behavior without prompting by the handler. This is done with 100% reliability. (It is done correctly 10 times out of 10 exercises.)

Personal Notes:

# Step 5: Increasing the Size of the Search Area

The next step to the Wilderness Air Scent progression involves increasing the size of the search area...by slowly increasing the distance between the handler and helper. At this stage you are still doing precisely the same exercise as Step 4 but with a greater distance between the helper and handler until you have reached about 100 feet between the two. Then,

a. **Add a Right Turn:** Change the location of the training so that the search area includes an abrupt right turn into the bushes/woods/or behind some other cover. An ideal environment might be a dirt road along a stand of thin woods but thick enough so that when the helper darts into the woods, they are completely out of sight. The helper will only dart into the woods for a distance of about ten feet, just out of sight.

During this exercise, the handler will place the dog in a ready position. The helper begins at the handler in front of the dog, talking to the dog, keeping the dog's attention by flashing a high quality treat several feet in front of him and take off running, waving his arms and making noises to keep the attention of the dog as he goes down the path about 100 feet and darts into the woods.

The handler immediately gives the search command as soon as the helper is in the woods and watches the dog as he takes off running toward the helper. The dog will probably pass by the helper (who is hidden inside the woods line) and then, perhaps immediately, turn around and go into the helper as he learns to use his nose and picks up the scent of the human he was following. If the dog does not recognize that he is out of scent for the first few repetitions, have the helper to make a noise so the dog turns around and goes into the helper. It usually does not take but a few of these repetitions before the light bulb turns on and the dog begins to use his nose...IF the handler has set up the problem correctly with the wind blowing directly from the helper to the handler at the beginning of the exercise. If the problem is set up in reverse, it will most likely not happen.

b. **Add a Left Turn:** Do the same exercise but begin to add a left turn.

c. **Alternate right and left turns into the woods.**

d. **Move into the woods to begin the problem.** Begin to have the helper begin at the edge of a path and dart directly into the woods with the dog watching the helper leave the path just a few feet in front of him and darting into the woods where he will then still make either a right or left turn once into the woods about 100 feet.

e. **Change the location to introduce the dog to various environments.**

f. **The helper begins the exercise about 50 feet away from the dog instead of right in front of the dog.** However, the dog can still visually see the helper leave and turn into the brush where he becomes invisible.

g. **The helper begins the exercise out of sight of the dog; however,** the scent is still available from the dog to the helper...a *hot* problem.

h. **Increase the size of the area to search.** Begin to increase the size of the search area to a rectangle of about 1 acre, slowly and gradually increasing the size of the search area to 40 acres. This is not something done overnight and if done too quickly will result in a dog totally confused and unsuccessful.

It is recommended that each of the above steps be done over the course of several months. These exercises are still using what we refer to as *hot trails* or a *hot problem* (since they are not actually trailing training but the dog is in essence trailing the person to the location, although not required to put his nose on the ground and actually learning to air scent in the process.) If the dog is unsuccessful in any of these steps, go back to the previous step until the dog is successful and introduce the next step in a smaller increment until the dog is successful. Do not mix up the sequence of the exercises *a* through *h* and do not try to move from one exercise to the next without mastering the previous one. You will only end up backtracking to re-teach the unlearned and unreliable step. Make sure each is solid before moving to the next.

Each of the steps should be repeated as noted below:

**Frequency:** Repeat each step of this exercise 4-5 times in a row before moving to the next suggestion on a different day. Always end the exercise on a positive note with the dog being successful. Do this for 6 days in a row, preferably twice a day for a total of 24 – 30 repetitions.

**Definition of Success:** The dog reliably leaves the handler when given the "find" command and runs to the helper. The dog turns around in short order (within 45 seconds) and returns to the handler. The handler tells the dog to "show me" and the dog immediately turns back around and returns to the helper. This is done with 100% reliability. (It is done correctly 10 times out of 10 exercises.)

Personal Notes:

_____

_____

_____

_____

_____

_____

_____

_____

_____

_____

_____

_____

_____

_____

_____

_____

_____

_____

_____

_____

_____

_____

_____

_____

_____

_____

_____

_____

_____

_____

_____

_____

# Step 6: Move to Cold Problems

The next step involves moving from a *"hot problem"* to a *"cold problem."* This means that the dog will no longer watch the victim go into the woods and the beginning location of the helper will not be in or near the immediate vicinity of the dog; hence, there will be no scent for the dog to "trail." This will require the dog to begin the problem searching for the person using a search strategy defined by the handler. This could be walking down a path until the dog reaches the scent of the person coming from the edge of the woods or any of many other possible scenarios. It means that the helper will enter the search area from another direction other than the one the handler/dog team plans to use.

At this point, the handler needs to have a plan on how they will search the area and begin the search mission with the dog using the same start procedures in an area where there is literally no scent of the helper in the immediate vicinity. However, the problem must be set up so that the dog will encounter that scent cone in short order and continue to go in to the helper demonstrating the refind process. If the problem is set up correctly, the dog should have no problem mastering this step in short order.

If the dog is not successful with this move from a hot problem to a cold problem, think about the cause of that confusion to determine what needs to be changed to set up a successful problem. Some typical causes of an unsuccessful transition to cold problems might include:

a. The wind is blowing in the opposite direction and blowing the scent cone away from the handler/dog team.

b. There is no wind blowing and the scent cone has not yet reached the dog.

c. The dog does not understand the search process; the handler should return to the previous step.

d. The handler is not executing a search strategy. (Handler needs to have a plan on how the area will be covered and proceed with that plan. The handler does not just sit back and watch the dog...but walks in a planned manner encouraging the dog to work in front of the handler moving from side-to-side in a zigzag type of pattern to cover the area. This teaches the dog to zigzag and they will begin to do this maneuver quite naturally in the future. At this stage of the game if the handler just walks a straight line, the dog may learn to just walk a straight line.)

If there is a problem, try implementing the 'check it' command and ask the dog to check it on the right, then move to the left and 'check it' on the left side, demonstrating a zig-zag fashion of searching. Eventually you will extinguish the check it commands and the dog should continue checking in a zig-zag pattern.

In addition, the handler should not walk right up on the dog...or try running behind the dog. If you need to stay on top of your dog, perhaps you do not need one. Just walk the whole area yourself. Stay behind the dog a good ways (30-50 feet) and trust that your dog will return to you once he has found the helper. If you are afraid of losing your dog, neither you nor your dog is ready for this step.

*Watch your dog* in all phases of training. When the dog reaches the scent cone, he should head in the direction of the cone with the handler stopping and waiting for the dog to return with the indication and refind to the helper. Watch the dog closely to determine when he has gotten into scent and you will be on your way to having a detailed communication system with your partner. Do the ears perk up? Does he stop for a few seconds and intently stare into a certain direction? Does his nose go into the air? Does his tail stop wagging? Start wagging? Go up? Go down? Watch your dog for subtle clues that he is in scent. Or leaving scent...

During this stage it is helpful to have *radio communication* with the helper and to know exactly where the helper has hidden. In this way you will avoid guiding your dog directly 'to' the helper or directly 'away' from the helper when they have caught the scent cone.

When the dog catches the edge of the scent cone, the handler will abandon the planned search strategy, take note of exactly where they are leaving the pattern of searching (in case they need to return to the area to properly cover the area) and either temporarily stop, allowing the dog to pursue the scent cone in whatever direction he chooses while you await his return and the indication behavior, or slowly move in the direction of the dog if the helper is a larger distance from you at that time but not fast enough to catch up to the dog or get into the visual zone of the helper.

The exercise is not for you to keep up with your dog, it is for the dog to find the helper and return to you to let you know they have found the person, perform their indication behavior, and take you to the helper. Do not even try to keep up with the dog as that will likely interfere with the sequence.

Also during this stage, it is important to maintain a reasonable distance from the helper at all times. Dogs are smart, and when the dog finds the helper and turns to return to you, if you are in a close visual distance from the helper and the dog surmises that you can see the helper (yeah, yeah, I know we do not know exactly what the dog is thinking but our experiences have shown us this phenomenon many times.) You may not get your return, indication behavior, and completed sequence if you are right on top of the dog and helper. Slow down and allow the dog to do his job without the interference of *you* being too close.

At this time the handler can begin to expand the search area to 40 – 60 acres, using a varied terrain, correct scenting winds, and proper search strategy. When the handler has mastered the daylight search, begin to practice at night moving from dusk into darkness using lighted collars and headlights on your hat. The dog will now get used to seeing lights in the woods, encountering nightlife, and may work a bit slower in that scenario. Avoid shining flashlights and headlights in the face of the dog or fellow flankers. Temporarily blinding your dog or flanker does not make you a valued crew member. Note: Some Wilderness Air Scent tests require a day and a night problem for certification while others only require a daylight test.

You are entering the *Trust your Dog* stage and you will move from *you* being the instructor and knowing where the helper is at all times, to doing some blind problems...not knowing exactly where the helper is located but having a defined search area to search.

**Frequency:** Repeat this exercise until the dog understands and repeatedly performs the indication behavior upon return to the handler without a prompting on a cold problem. Always end the exercise on a positive note with the dog being successful, even if you have to prompt that indication. Do this for 6 days in a row, preferably twice a day for a total of 24 – 30 repetitions.

**Definition of Success:** The dog reliably performs the indication behavior without prompting by the handler in a cold problem. This is done with 100% reliability. (It is done correctly 10 times out of 10 exercises.)

Personal Notes:
_____
_____
_____
_____
_____
_____
_____
_____

# Step 7: Add Variety

After completing step 6, begin to practice with a variety of terrains, variety of victims (ages, races, disabilities, wheelchairs, walkers, running, walking, laying on the ground, standing up, in plain view, hidden, up in a tree, underneath a tarp, hidden in a vehicle, hidden in a building, buried in leaves, or anything else you can concoct.) Begin to include a variety of helper behaviors as well...afraid of the dog, happy to see the dog, drunk acting/slurred speech, scared, depressed, responsive and nonresponsive. Think of the 90 year old Alzheimer's missing person and their frailty, a two-year old child's response, and everything in between.

Then try having the helper to move from one place to another once the dog has been in the first time. It is priceless to watch the eyes of the dog who has found someone, returned to the handler, given his indication, the handler following the dog on the refind in a timely manner and the subject not there. This requires the dog to re-find the person and do it all over again. If the dog responds by giving up instead of continuing to search, have the victim/helper to make a noise to refocus the dog, or have the handler to re-start the dog on what will now be a hot trail or hot problem.

Remember to always look up, look around, look inside, and look down, to the right, to the left, and behind you as you search. The missing person could be anywhere and major clues may be just ahead. It is amusing to watch a dog figure out that the helper is now up in the tree stand. They may actually try to climb the stairs. There seems to be no limit to the capabilities of the dog given appropriate training and experience. However, the handler must remember to select a search strategy...it is not just going into the woods to 'look.' It is going into an assigned search segment with boundaries which are recognizable and 'covering' your area in a manner which will put the least likelihood that the missing person is in fact in your search segment and you did not find him.

Personal Notes:

_____

_____

_____

_____

_____

_____

_____

_____

# Step 8: Moving into More Challenging Search Environments

Once the dog has mastered a smaller area, select larger areas, slowly increasing the size of the area and the time needed for searching the area. Do not get hooked into always searching a small area. You need to train like you would search...with gear and conditions. So now is the time to provide additional environments and search sizes...taking one modification at a time and encouraging the dog to experience a wider variety of conditions. •

The following is a list of ideas to consider when expanding the training of the Air Scent dog:

• *Increase the size of the area*: Then begin to increase the size larger and larger until you reached 40 to 60 acres. Most certification tests place a victim in an environment about that size.

• *Brush density:* Increase the density of the area, but at this stage of the training handlers should not include extreme terrain such as thick briars, swamp, or other hazardous environments.

• *Building Search*: Begin with a small storage building. When doing building searches there are two main approaches to searching an enclosed area. First you must determine if the structure is safe. If the structure is not safe, the handler would ask the dog to enter the building and observe, as best as possible without entering the structure, what areas the dog has searched. The dog will enter the building and try to identify/isolate the scent inside. In a small storage room, the space is limited and there is usually no air conditioning/heater, etc. This is the simplest introduction to buildings. However, if the building is in such a condition that it might injure your dog, decline the invitation to search the structure. Consider coving the victim with a tarp or large card board box so it is not a visual find.

• *Directed vs. Self directed Search*: If the structure is safe for the handler to enter the handler may do so and provide a directed search activity for the dog. In this manner, the handler stays to the right of the room, following the wall around the room, pointing to each section of the room asking the dog to "check it." As the dog checks an area and leaves it, the handler moves with the wall around the room to check all areas, including vents, high locations, low locations, furniture, drawers, etc. After working their way around the room, allow the dog ample time to return to any area he showed some interest in the first pass. In a small room, you will usually not have a re-find, even if the dog has been taught to do a re-find. You will still have the alert/indication at the victim or as close to the scent source as the dog can get if the victim is out of reach such as on the roof top or in the attic.

Some handlers prefer to allow the dog to search a building/room self-directed first and observe any indication or slight behavior change, extra sniff or prolonged interest in an area before performing any type of directed search or "check it" commands. In a self-directed search by the dog, the handler will remain at the doorway or entryway of the building/room and allow the dog to independently explore the room and locate any scent. (This is usually done by an experienced dog who definitively understands the command to find live scent or human remains and uses his nose to search the area assigned.) If all is visible, the handler should note any areas not searched by the dog and consider directing the dog to those areas to be sure they are not concealing the victim or HRD. Watch for very small nuances in the dog behavior and explore any of those locations to the fullest extent possible.

It is entirely up to the hander what type of approach they wish to use which may change from scene to scene based upon a myriad of factors. It is fine to use both approaches.

● *Residential homes*: Use a directed search strategy for residential homes encouraging the dog to check closets, under furniture, vents, etc. It is helpful to turn off the air conditioning and heating system and allow the home to "rest" for 20 or 30 minutes before searching if possible. Remember that an air conditioning system can easily blow the scent all around. Do not forget to check attics, crawl spaces, and inside and under all furniture. Also check under the covers/blankets on a bed, especially for small children. Check inside toy boxes and underneath tarps, laundry baskets, underneath sinks, etc. Just where you think they could not possibly fit, they will be found.

● *Rubble:* In cases of rubble, regardless of the cause, safety is paramount. If you do not feel it is safe for your dog to work a rubble pile, do not do it. Of necessity, is having your dog to train on rubble and feeling confident that you can direct your dog from the bottom (right, left, come, back, etc.) while you are on the ground level and your dog is high on the rubble and possibly far enough away that he cannot hear you over the other tractors and generator noises which will be present on an actual site. Be sure to teach a "slow" command to encourage the dog to slow down when appropriate. It can make traversing the rubble much safer.

Finding these challenging environments is only limited by your imagination and access to various scenarios. Be ever vigilant when a motel is due for destruction, or other large buildings or scene may allow you to train on their premises. One team trains on rubble at a concrete disposal site...ever changing and absolutely a real-life site. However, always ask permission and use personal protective gear such as steel-toed boots, knee pads, eye protection, and appropriate techniques.

## Cross Training a Wilderness Air Scent Dog with Human Remains Detection

There is controversy over whether it is efficient, prudent, and wise to use a cross-trained dog for rubble work. A cross-trained dog is one which is trained to find both live Air Scent and Human Remains. The main goal in a rubble search is initially to find all live victims. Rescuers would prefer not to use valuable time, energy and resources to recover bodies if there is a possibility of live victims needing assistance.

It is always wise for a handler to know what the dog normally does when given the live command when there is cadaver material in the search area and vice versa. That is not to say that the dog would perform this behavior every time, but might give the handler a clue as to what the dog is trying to tell him when a real life scene includes both live and deceased.

Rubble work also involves prior training for a dog to "leave it" and ignore common distracters like bags of dog food and frozen chicken or hot dogs. Never allow a dog to eat anything at a rubble site or in the field. It is likely contaminated. This includes deer bones or other scatter.

In addition, consider the extra time involved in training in more than one discipline. Twice the training, logs, equipment, etc. However, also consider what resources are available in your area and what the majority of callout requests will entail. Is there a need for a cadaver dog in addition to a wilderness air scent live find dog? All of this comes into play when making the "cross training decision." And lastly but not least, consider the legalities of a cross-trained dog in the courtroom. This is covered in quite some detail in the book co-authored by this author, Training a Human Remains Detection Dog.

By all means, the dog should be agile, healthy, and comfortable working on unsteady surfaces having been exposed to many types of unstable surfaces prior to training on rubble. These first responder dogs are usually local teams who are first on site after a disaster and like the firemen and other first responders on scene almost immediately. They are often the ones to locate live victims prior to trained disaster dogs arriving on scene. Remember to train for this if you intend to respond to this type of environment and know when to say "no" if the disaster is out of the realm of your training experiences.  In the least, do no harm.

Figure 51 K9 Gibbs.  Handler: Christy Judah.  First time for Gibbs on a rubble pile.

Figure 52 K9 Beau. Handler: Wendy Long.  An experienced team.

## Cross-training a Wilderness Air Scent Dog

If you decide to add HRD (Human Remains Detection) to the Wilderness Air Scent dog training...it is highly suggested that you complete the Wilderness Air Scent training to the point of certification prior to adding the HRD to the repertoire. Once you are WAS certified, then...consider the following:

There are many opinions regarding training techniques for cadaver dogs and the level of threshold[22] or amount of odor used in training. Some folks feel smaller amounts, such as just blood, is not worth training as it would also include menstrual items, cutting yourself shaving, etc. Others specialize in forensics work, with minute amounts, or historic work, using dry bone as the source material. This author has found no problems using a variety of materials, amounts, age, types, etc. in training but would recommend using bloody tissue to begin the training. Others have begun with dry bone and added tissue in later trainings. Both methods work. Later in the training, dry bone, just blood, or other parts may be introduced in various quantities. For now, concentrate on one source odor and add other types of source material and larger amounts at a later stage of training. In HRD training, the *amount* of material used is referred to as the "threshold" of the source material...from small amounts to an entire body. Eventually, be sure your dog is exposed to various thresholds. If you do not train on larger amounts from time to time, your dog may very well fringe – even 100 feet away from the body and refuse to enter the more intense smelling area. Do not be baffled, but recognize when your dog is fringing. A dog exposed to a full body may not choose to approach it in close proximity; he may be overwhelmed with the scent.

## Imprinting

Begin HRD training by exposing the dog to the odor of HR, often called 'imprinting.' Imprinting is usually done on lead so that you have total control over where the dog will go next. It is important to spend the same amount of time at each location so as not to unintentionally train your dog to alert where you linger longer. Exercises which imprint the odor of human remains might include:

---

[22] Threshold: the minimum intensity of a stimulus that is detected by a particular dog. It can be affected by climate as well as internal and external environmental factors. SWGDOG.     http://swgdog.fiu.edu/approved-guidelines/sc1_terminology_abcdefghijk.pdf

a. Gather about ten containers...such as new, unused paint cans or coffee cans, and place them in a circle. Add source material into three of the cans. Walk the dog around the circle allowing him to "check" each of the cans. When he reaches the can with the source inside and lingers just a second longer than the other cans, say, "good Koli" or whatever word you have assigned to mean human remains. Reward as appropriate...which can easily be a food reward (of high caliber such as pieces of chicken)...and offered immediately at the source or as near the source as possible without touching the source material.

b. Use ten concrete blocks to create a circle or line of the same exercise as above. However, start the dog from different ends of the line or circle so as not to pattern train. (i.e. do not teach the dog that in every third block is a source; vary the amount of blocks between sources.)

c. After the dog learns to expect a reward at the source, and it is pretty obvious to you that the dog understands the odor of human remains, begin asking for an alert/final response behavior at the source. Example: Walk around the circle, dog sniffs the source and looks at you for a reward, you immediately say "sit" and reward the dog at source. Timing is critical with this...no hesitation on your part and have the food reward ready to go.

## Small Area Training

Once you have determined that the dog understands the odor, and is offering the final response behavior (sit) at the source, it is time to expand the size of the area of training. Begin by using a 10 X 10 area and:

1. Place the dog in a *ready position*.

2. Give the search command such as "find koli."

3. Release the dog to go in front of you to search.

4. Once the dog reaches the source and sits at source, reward. (If you need to remind the dog to sit as you watch from the distance, do so until the dog ultimately sits automatically.

115

Slowly enlarge the search area, but concentrate more on refining and cementing the final response behavior. As you begin to search larger areas, and thus are further away from your dog, the dog may revert back to a refind behavior to bring you into the area where the remains are located. In this case, praise your dog for the refind, and hurriedly run behind your dog to the odor source. The dog should take you to the source and then immediately offer the final response. Reward the dog immediately.

Begin to include various environments, buildings, buried, hanging, and any other type of scenario you can create. When burying source material, be sure to dig additional distracter holes so the dog does not alert on the freshly dug dirt. Refer to further reading for more training tips.

To summarize, in the Human Remains Detection progression, the steps (incorporating a refind) include:

1. The handler decides whether to work the area on lead or off lead depending upon the scene, terrain and conditions.

2. The handler gives the search command and the dog begins to methodically search for the scent of human remains.

3. The dog finds the scent of human remains, and based upon training either alerts to the scent/location, staying with the strongest source of scent, or returns to the handler doing a refind.

4. The dog indicates to the handler with a trained behavior (alert/indication) that he has found the scent of human remains (either remaining with the scent source or returning to the handler.)

5. If the dog has returned to the handler (done a refind) then the handler tells the dog to "show me" and the dog returns to the strongest source of the scent.

6. The handler follows the dog to the source of the scent which may or may not be visible to the handler.

7. The dog completes a trained final response in close proximity to the source of scent such as a sit or a down.

8. The handler rewards the dog.

Remember that with any training, some dogs are not suited for human remains detection. They may have an aversion to the odor of human remains and not wish to add this discipline to their training. You should be able to recognize a dog aversion to this scent when they refuse to approach the scent, shy away from the scent, turn their head away from the scent, or walk away from the scent. In this case, do not force the dog to "like" working human remains detection. Instead, be happy with your Wilderness Air Scent dog and keep looking for the living. You will have exposed your dog to the scent of HR and should be able to recognize this aversive behavior in the woods. This is another clue to you that your dog has detected something, even if you do not get the final trained response or they take you to the deceased. In any case, practice will help you to recognize these behaviors and you should occasionally add HRD to the environment when working live exercises.

This introduction to HRD training is just that, a very brief introduction and serious handlers who decide to cross-train are encouraged to seek out additional training information in the <u>Training a Human Remains Detection Dog</u>. That book will provide much more specific details, incorporate toy rewards, and provide a complete framework for HRD work.

## Probability of Detection

Handlers may be asked to put an estimate, or *probability of detection*, on each completed assignment by reporting a number…your POD number when you return to base camp. In the simplest of terms, if there were ten playing cards in your search segment, how many do you suppose you would have found? Three out of ten? That would be a 30% POD or probability of detection (POD) that you would have found the missing person if they are in fact inside your assigned search segment.

Only a search segment where every single foot of the terrain is visible to the handler should receive a 100% POD…and that even discounts that the victim may indeed be buried on the property. If the victim is located, then the handler may provide a 100% POD and only in those circumstances. Otherwise, consider a very conservative POD unless you have reason to provide a higher one. This number may be used by the planning and operations personnel to decide whether to place additional teams of searchers in this area and in combination with their POD decide to move to other search areas if the victim is not found. Do not take this estimate lightly. Be honest and forthright with any areas not searched at all (perhaps due to hazards) or overlooked by handlers or dogs. Never talk yourself out of searching an area because the victim "just wouldn't have gone in there." It is a high likelihood that this is exactly where they are waiting, hurt, disoriented or just plain lost.

Note: There are very complicated and detailed methods for calculating probability of detection other than the simplistic one noted above. Interested readers should pursue additional writings on this topic to further understand more scientific and research based methods of determining POD. For this authors use, the description above has sufficed. She would rather underestimate than overestimate her POD...and in most cases rarely volunteers her POD unless asked.

## Trust Your Dog

Figure 53 K9 Cirque. Handler: Craig Veldheer. Puppy Focus.

Figure 54 K9 Cirque.  Handler:  Craig Veldheer.

Figure 55 K9 Ayla.  Handler:  Pam Bennett.

Figure 56 K9 Orion. Handler: Kim Veldheer.

Figure 57 K9 Tigger.  Handler:  Kim Veldheer.

Figure 58 K9 Binka.  Handler:  Shelley Wood.

Figure 59 K9 Nicholas.  Handler:  Aleta Aldridge.

Chapter Seven

# Search Strategies and Scent Specific Dogs

**Objectives**

*Understand the difference between Scent-specific and non-scent specific wilderness air scent dogs.*

*Be able to recognize terrain features and plan an effective search strategy.*

---

In training, if using a cross-trained dog, it is helpful to provide environments with both scent sources available and to observe what the dog will do when given one command with both scent sources in the search area. It is also recommended to provide training situations when the dog is given one command but the other scent is present in the search area. Only through extensive training and varying the training scenarios, can a handler interpret as many of the dog behaviors as possible.

## Scent Specific Air Scent Dogs

Scent-specific air scent dogs usually refers to an air scent dog being able to differentiate between individuals. In this case, the dog is given a scent article (which has been correctly collected...see appendix for techniques) and asked to find only one specific person. To train a scent specific air scent dog, one begins by placing a "good" scent article on the ground beside the dog, not calling attention to it, but just laying it beside the dog before beginning the initial training exercises. As you progress through the training and get to the stage where the dog will be leaving the handler and looking for the subject, ask the dog to "check it" with a wide sweep of your hand toward the scent article (refer to the appendix for collecting scent articles without contaminating them.)  The K9 knows your particular scent, but you should avoid putting your scent on the scent article as other handlers may need to use the same scent article at a later time.

After the dog has "checked it," give the search command.  You can almost see a light bulb flash when the dog picks up the idea that, "oh, yes, we are looking for *that* scent." During these exercises, be SURE the wind direction is blowing into the face of the dog so that they *can* make that distinction.

As the dog begins to use his nose and not his eyes to find the victim...and believe me, you will notice, be sure that all problems are set up properly so that you are not inadvertently training the dog to do something other than the desired outcome.  When you inadvertently train the dog to do something you did not want him to do, it is called *accidental training*.  Teammates and experienced trainers can alert you to little nuances you are doing that may be classified as *unintentional or accidental training*.

Eventually you will add a scent discrimination problem in the mix...by asking two individuals to walk away without the dog watching, and about 50 feet down the trail, they split paths walking in opposite directions.  Providing the scent article, watch how the dog reacts when the trail splits, and praise heavily if the dog follows the correct scent path to the desired victim.  If the dog turns and goes toward the wrong person, evaluate the problem set-up to determine if it is a poorly set up exercise or a lack of understanding on the part of the dog.  If the latter, back up a few steps, cement those steps, and try again later.

The process in the scent discrimination air scent dog uses a 'hot' problem.  This means that the scent of the person is at or close to the start location of the dog.  After the dog understands the process, problems should become "cold" meaning that the dog is started at a location where the subject scent is not reasonably expected to be. (I.e. the subject entered the woods or building from another location.)  And the second person whose scent is not on the scent article also entered the environment from another location than the handler and dog.  Remember...in essence, with the hot problem, you are asking the dog to 'trail' to the person but use the air scent rather than the scent which has fallen on the ground, crushed vegetation, etc.  We have no way of knowing which scent the dog is using to differentiate between the two victims...as the scent used for trailing is laid onto the trail the same way.  During air scent discrimination exercises...the goal is to teach the dog that the scent belongs to a particular person...not just any human.  As the exercises become longer and more difficult, there will also be 'cold' problems with two subjects in the woods...both entering the woods from a different location so the dog does not in essence trail to the person.  These exercises mimic teaching trailing in some aspects but do not produce a true trailing dog; rather add another tool to the handler's tool chest in being able to determine if the dog is capable and trained to find a particular person and not just any person in the area. The ultimate goal is to find the missing person.

Wilderness Air Scent dogs do not have to be scent specific. If the dog finds other people in the woods (not the missing person) it is fine...question those folks to see if they have seen the missing person and proceed with reporting appropriate new information to the command center. They may have just seen or know something which may assist the planning and operations personnel in the command center; or may encounter some clue or evidence which may help later. It is truly amazing to watch a well-trained air scent dog work a cone and demonstrate his trained indication upon a find and so rewarding to know a job was well done.

## Common Search Strategies

Searching is not just heading to the woods or search area and looking around. The search strategy must be planned and efficient taking into account environment, safety, situation, missing person characteristics, weather, wind speed, size of search area, and a myriad of additional factors. Basically, a searcher is assigned a specific area to search with his dog and flanking crew. Based upon wind direction, if possible, select an appropriate technique to ensure maximum coverage in a timely manner under the current conditions. Some suggested techniques include a:

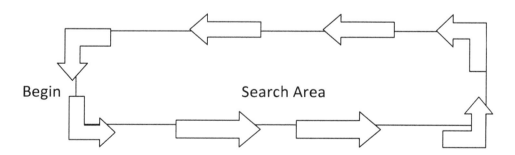

Figure 60 Perimeter Search.

127

1. **Perimeter search:** Search around the outside or just inside the search area. If searching a wooded area, it is always better to search just inside the tree line rather than on the path or open area surrounding it as it makes for better scent conditions for the dog. (And it is probably pretty obvious that the missing person is not on the path…you can pretty well eliminate that in short order without a dog. Even a flanker on the woods edge can also be checking the path as it winds in the woods without the dog handler being on the path directly.)

2. **Circular Pattern:** Begin with the "clue," "bone," or other item and proceed making circular patterns around as you expand the circle. Continue to expand around original location expanding your search area. This is helpful when a deceased body was located and removed; now law enforcement has asked you to locate additional bones, or other clues. Expand the search area as far as desired depending upon terrain.

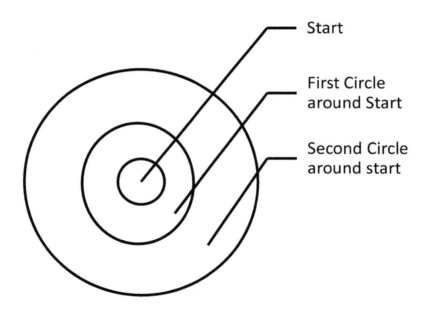

Start

First Circle around Start

Second Circle around start

Interestingly if we look at the patterns which homing pigeons use, as illustrated in the late 1800s, we find several variations of the circular search pattern.

Figure 61 Homing Pigeons Search Patterns.

23

3. **Grid Method:** During the grid method, a direction of travel is planned with specified spacing based upon terrain features...i.e. the more dense the terrain, the closer the grid.

North

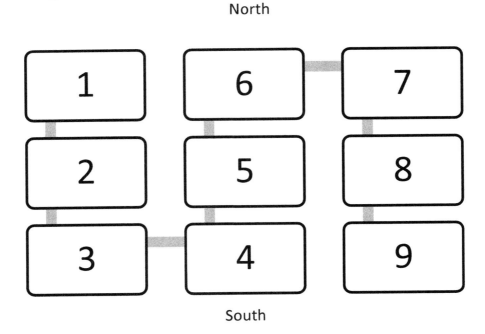

South

23 Homing Pigeons Search patterns. File:PSM V44 D787 Homing pigeons search patterns.jpg 1893-1894. Popular Science Monthly, Volume 44. Author unknown.

After completing 1 through 9...begin to grid in the opposite direction starting at "1" and moving from west to east the second time through.  For instance begin at 1 and move to 6 – 7 – 8—5 –2 -- 3 – 4 – 9.  This ensures you have gridded to the most efficient coverage and is labor intensive but efficient if a close grid search is needed.

4.  **Zone Search:**  Divide the assigned search area into zones.  Search each one independently of the other and slowly cover the entire area.  Note that the area can be subdivided in any formation...does not have to be four equal quadrants.  Search strategy is heavily dependent upon terrain and density.  Select a pattern which optimizes your efforts.

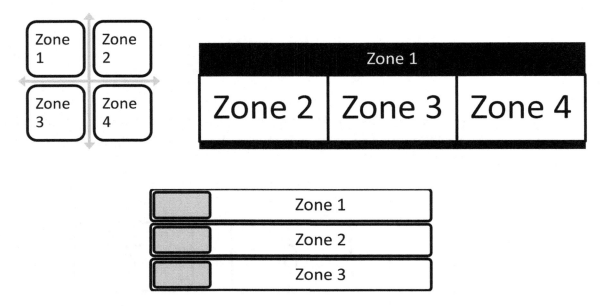

5.  **Hasty Search**:  Using search and rescue hasty search techniques (which you learned in your search and rescue technician classes) search main paths and small openings in the woods along the paths looking for tracks or clues.  Ask the dog to check it in each one...for a distance inside the woods line of perhaps 20 to 30 feet.  If they pick up a scent, they will go deeper and you leave your path to enter the woods at that location.  If within short order you do not locate the person, return to the path and continue your hasty search.

6.  **Guide Search:** Guide searches use a visible environmental focus to guide on...in other words, one person is within sight of the path through the woods.  The second person is one critical space (within sight of the original person and able to see halfway to the other person to ensure that all areas are covered and no clues

are missed. The third person is one critical space deeper from the second person and guides off of the second person. The entire line moves at an even pace with the pace set by the dog and handler who are searching ahead of the guide line by perhaps 10 to 20 feet or more depending upon the terrain. The guide line is behind the handler/dog at all times. The handler focuses on walking directly in front of the guide line watching his dog and ensuring that the dog is quartering the terrain in front of him. At times, the handler may ask the line to stop or 'hold' for the dog to finish searching a certain area.

This is sometimes called a **line search.** A **line search** occurs when a group of searchers (perhaps six?) line up in a straight line, one critical space apart (whereby they can see half way to the person beside them to search the ground pretty thoroughly), and proceed to move through the terrain in a pace which maintains the line. Hence, line search technique.

7.  Any other formation that the terrain dictates. The choices of a search strategy are only limited by the imagination of the handler and the terrain assigned. Use whatever technique gives the dog the greatest advantage to find the person if the person is indeed located in your assigned segment. However, whatever strategy you select needs to be documented on maps and reported back to the planning/operations personnel during debriefing (the summary you provide to the search command staff regarding your activities after completing your assigned mission.) Here is an example where the beginning is set (based on clues or assigned area) and for whatever reason you are asked to search the northern section of this area...

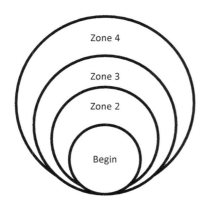

Many different strategies could be employed to cover these areas; whatever works for that day.

*Notes:*

132

Figure 62 K9 Hope.  Handler:  Chris Holmberg.

------------------

*Cherish all your happy moments: they make a fine cushion for old age.*

**Christopher Morley (1890 - 1957)**

------------------

**Chapter Eight**

# Crime Scene Preservation and Critical Incident Stress Debriefing

## Objectives

*Be able to list several crime scene preservation recommendations.*

*Be able to list various types of evidence which may be present at a crime scene.*

*Understand the importance of recognizing stress that is a result of a traumatic or search experience.*

*Recognize symptoms of distress in yourself and your team mates that may occur as a result of search experiences.*

*Understand how to request and participate in a Critical Incident Stress Debriefing.*

## Crime Scene Preservation

What is a crime scene? Any search scene is a potential crime scene. This means that you need to

*Protect the Crime Scene to preserve all physical evidence.*

search and understand that clues are everywhere and they must be preserved in case this search mission becomes a crime scene. What are clues? Everything is a clue...the grass, the trees, flowers, stones, limbs, trash, blood, body parts, full bodies, clothing, food containers, drink bottles, etc. Everything will be looked at for any impact or lack of impact on the crime itself. Therefore, searchers need to be cognizant of not destroying any evidence. They also need to inform law enforcement if they have touched, rearranged, moved or in any other way altered the environment in a crime scene.

If you have found yourself in a crime scene, unless there is some reason for you to remain there (such as providing immediate first aide, cardiopulmonary resuscitation, etc.), back out the same way you entered the area and flag off a distance of at least 25 feet around the scene with flagging tape. Keep any other individuals from entering the area until the law enforcement official assumes control of the scene.

Helpful definitions:

Crime Scene: any physical location where you suspect or know that a crime has occurred.
Primary Crime Scene: the location where the crime actually occurred.
Secondary Crime Scene: the location where potential clues may be found regarding the crime.
Trace evidence: such as hair, fiber or skin cells.

Various types of evidence might include:

- Ballistics: bullet casings, bullets, weapons, gun powder
- Biology/DNA: blood, body fluids, semen, saliva
- Documents: any written or ink evidence
- Drugs: any controlled substances
- Latent prints: feet, shoes, fingers, ears, lips, tire tread, etc.
- Microscopic Evidence: hair, fiber, skin cells, fiber, soil, etc.
- Tool marks: such as left by a hammer, screw driver, etc.
- Toxicology evidence: blood or tissue containing drug evidence or poisons

Protect the crime scene from any changes which may occur since you discovered it. Avoid touching anything. Avoid smoking or eating or drinking at the scene. Avoid using the phone at the scene. Do not use the toilet, turn on water, use towels, or otherwise touch anything at the scene. Do not discuss the scene with witnesses or bystanders. Refrain from touching or moving anything.

Of importance is not to ADD anything to the search segment or potential crime scene. Do not drop gum papers, drink bottles, tissue, cigarette butts, or anything else in the search area whether it is a known crime scene or not. Do not leave any evidence of you!

Make note of all details you observed. Note the weather conditions, humidity, temperature, and wind direction and whether the ground is wet or dry. Note location of obvious key evidence without touching it...such as a weapon, hammer, etc. Once law enforcement has taken over, remove yourself from the scene...your mission is complete.

## Critical Incident Stress Debriefing[24]

On a final note, handlers need to become aware of where CISD debriefing is available and seek out that service when needed. Viewing a death scene is something that will become emblazoned onto your mind's eye and can affect even the most seasoned and experienced handler in damaging and negative ways. Sleep disturbances, marital or family difficulties, work difficulties, loss of appetite or eating too much, irritability, depression, drugs/alcohol usage, withdrawal from others, and many other symptoms can present after a stressful or disturbing experience.

Most communities offer CISD counseling or debriefing to first responders at no charge. Ask your local emergency manager, health department, or law enforcement agency for contact information on services available in your area. Most CISD opportunities allow the responders to gather either individually or within a group of those who shared your experience, to discuss and find out what others saw or how they are feeling about the same experience, and create a plan to positively handle your thoughts and feelings. It is no shame or weakness to recognize that we are all human and need that positive interaction to handle such extraordinary events in our lives in order to continue to do this work in the long run. Ask your team chief or other local personnel to find a source for a CISD counselor who will be available to conduct a meeting or individual session with you. You are the most important consideration...take care of YOU.[25]

*Very little is needed to make a happy life.*
**Marcus Aurelius Antoninus (121 AD - 180 AD)**, *Meditations*

---

[24] International Critical Incident Stress Foundation. http://www.icisf.org/ Check the web site for various regional offices.
[25] Mitchell, Jeffrey T. Critical incident Stress Debriefing. American Academy of Experts in Traumatic Stress. University of Maryland. http://www.info-trauma.org/flash/media-e/mitchellCriticalIncidentStressDebriefing.pdf

*No man is happy who does not think himself so.*
**Publilius Syrus (~100 BC)**, *Maxims*

# Chapter Nine

# Certification, Ethics and Recordkeeping

## Objectives

*Understand the importance
of keeping training and search records.*

*Describe the steps to setting up
a fair and ethical Canine Evaluation.*

*Recognize and adopt
ethical practices in search and rescue.*

## Train Regularly and Keep Logs

All search and rescue dogs should be trained on a regular basis. Currently, in the law enforcement field, this means a minimum of sixteen hours per month. This training should be documented in some type of log book whether electronic or paper and maintained for the career of the K9 team, the handler and dog. Cases can be prosecuted years after the fact. Don't be caught short.

Documentation of training exercises can be as simple as a spiral notebook or as complex as a computer generated and quite detailed report. Whatever method you chose, make plans for computer crashes and loss of data on any electronic means of recordkeeping. Many teams and departments choose to print out all records and keep paper copies in addition to electronic memory sticks or other means of backup.

Logs serve several purposes. First and foremost they help the handler maintain an accurate record of the training progression of the dog, document areas of strength or weakness, provide a glimpse into what future training goals might need to be, and offer a written document to the courtroom officials to verify that your dog is qualified, reliable and trained. As no K9 team is perfect, training logs should reflect any weaknesses, followed by remedial training, followed by successful completion. These three considerations will normally provide the documentation that you are in fact a trained and reliable witness if your testimony is needed in a court case.

Included in the appendix is a copy of a blank log sheet which is adequate to document training information and can be used or altered to serve any search and rescue handler purpose. Many teams are happy to share their adapted log forms, just ask. The form is not important. The importance lies in keeping some type of log book or documentation of your training.

## Deployment Requests

All search dogs deployed on an official search, as requested by law enforcement, emergency management, wildlife officials, or other official and legal entities, should be certified in the area where they are expected and requested to perform. It is generally recognized in the world of SAR that all missing person cases are a 'crime scene' until otherwise determined, and therefore a missing person callout is usually under the jurisdiction of law enforcement personnel. Volunteer SAR dog handlers are requested through an official callout system; whether by LEO, emergency management, or other agencies working with LEO.

In some states, missing person cases are managed by park officials or wildlife officers. Determine who the official entity of the missing person case is (which may vary based upon terrain) and respond to requests made by those agencies or organizations.

It is not wise to respond to search requests by family members...they may be asking you to search in the backyard of the subject who is suspected of killing the missing person. This is in direct conflict with police investigations, surveillance which may be in place, or the safety of the handler and dog. It is highly encouraged that any searcher who is contacted by the family intensely evaluates the situation, contact the investigator in charge of the case to ask permission, advice, and direction before responding to any family or private organization request.

Only consider those requests which allow you to respond to a terrain and type of scene that you are trained and certified to search. Just because your dog is certified in one discipline does not mean you are qualified to respond to a completely different discipline. In other words…if you are certified in Human Remains, you are not qualified to try to "trail" a person from a vehicle to their location or search for a person who is presumably still alive in a rubble scenario. Although we can never know when a person has moved from a live search scene to a recovery or human remains search, it is not our call to do so…it is the responsibility of law enforcement or other command staff to determine if and when a wilderness live find or a cadaver dog is needed. The same does not hold true for cross-trained dogs. Cross-trained dogs are those who can and do search for either live or deceased and can be deployed during any missing person event regardless of the unknown or known condition of the person.

## Certification of SAR Dogs

Dog teams (one dog and one handler) should be tested on a regular basis to document their continued skills in performing the predetermined tasks or discipline according to standards set forth by the local team, state officials, or other authorizing agency. These standards should be written and generally fall into line with other local, state or nationally recognized standards. However, due to costs involved in joining national organizations, and more importantly consideration of the costs involved in traveling great distances to national certification locations, it may be more prudent for local teams to develop their own canine standards in each discipline offered, train specific individuals to administer those tests, and offer those locally. Since many team members are volunteers, it makes good financial sense to locally and ethically administer certification tests. In the law enforcement field, this means a minimum of yearly, every 12 months, certification in every discipline in which the K9 team deploys. Other volunteer SAR teams re-certify each two years. Certification logs / records should be maintained for the career of the K9 team, the handler and dog. All certifications are conducted single-blind or double-blind (see below).

## Certifying Officials

The primary certifying official is one which is authorized by the agency or organization to perform a certification test or examinations documenting that the canine and handler have successfully performed to a set of predetermined standards. It is always good to have multiple individuals present at each testing to promote fair and ethical assessments. A minimum of two individuals should be present at every test. These certifying officials should be individuals who are accepted by a team as experienced searchers and have previously trained, worked and certified their own search and rescue dogs. It is one thing to be a good trainer. It is quite another to walk the walk, in this author's opinion; therefore, she recommends using evaluators which have trained and searched with their own certified SAR dog whenever possible and available.

## SAR Dog Tests: Single-blind vs. Double-blind

A single-blind test is one in which the dog handler and dog do not know the location of the missing subject. In this case, the certifying official or test administer knows the exact location of the subject. However, the locations is not identified by flagging tape or any other identifying clue which may assist the dog handler or dog to locate the subject.

In a double-blind test the certifying official nor the dog or dog handler know the location of the live subject. The subject is put into place by a person who is not present during the actual testing and has had no communication with the evaluator or dog handler to share the location of the live subject. No other person present or accompanying the evaluator or dog handler knows the location of the subject. In this case, the accuracy of the dog handler and dog performance is confirmed by the presence of the live subject and the observation of the dog doing the alert/indication and/or re-find if required as observed by the evaluator.

There is a controversy between proponents of both types of testing as to which is considered the most accurate and fair. Each team or organization will need to determine what best suits their needs. There are those who say that a fair and equitable test cannot be administered if even one person on the evaluation crew knows the location of the subject because of intentional or unintentional cues given by those who are aware of the location.

Others propose that in order to totally evaluate the handler and dog performance, the evaluator needs to know the location of the person. Using this approach they are able to more accurately assess whether the dog has indeed located the person according to training expectations, have missed the person, or are indifferent to the person. In addition, the evaluator can make a judgment call if an inordinate amount of time has passed and the dog and/or handler have missed the subject numerous times.  It can also provide information on whether the handler is accurately reading the dog in those cases when the evaluator can reasonably assess that the dog is 'in scent' or has shown no interest in the locations where the scent can plausibly be located.  Of course the evaluator cannot know for sure where the scent 'is' but can reasonably determine, based upon experience, knowledge of the location of the subject, wind, environmental conditions, and terrain, where the scent is most likely to be accessible to the dog.  Each agency or organization will determine what is in the best interests of their team. In the law enforcement field, certifications are conducted minimally single-blind.

## Proficiency Assessments

Proficiency assessments are similar to training, except proficiency assessments are conducted single-blind or double-blind. Therefore, proficiency assessments logs should be kept separate from training logs, reflecting blind testing. In the law enforcement field, the best practice is that proficiency assessments are conducted periodically. The frequency of periodic proficiency assessments are determined by the potential legal exposure of the K9 team's mission.  As an example, law enforcement explosives K9 proficiency assessments are conducted quite often, as the potential legal exposure of missing an explosive device is very high.  Each time during training that you work a blind problem, you are in essence taking a mini proficiency assessment.

## Setting Up the K9 Evaluation

Whether using single-blind, double-blind, or known certifications and training scenarios, all accompanying individuals should be aware of intentional or unintentional cuing of the dog and handler. The following is a list to consider when training or evaluating a dog team:

1. Select a date, time and location convenient to all parties.  Be vigilant and timely once the test is requested and planned.

2. Select an area that is not commonly used by the handler and dog. Set up the testing environment according to the size and terrain features described in the evaluation criteria. If the test calls for one acre for an HRD test, this should be one acre in an average terrain...not an extremely thick or extreme terrain. The same holds true for a wilderness air scent test...not an extreme terrain such as one full of briars or thick, thick brush. Be reasonable. Testing should be straight forward, not set up to trick the handler or dog. Testing should mirror actual deployment missions.

3. Place the training aids in an HRD test in a reasonable location. If the test encompasses an acre, do not place an odiferous tissue aid very near a dry bone source. The odor of the tissue will most likely overwhelm the faint smell of the dry bone and make for a very difficult, if not impossible, testing condition for the candidate. When setting up a test, be sure to use the entire area provided and separate the two or three sources across the area placing the smelliest aid in a position to not contaminate the less smelly aids. Take into consideration the amount and direction of the wind. If setting up a negative area (no source in the area), do not select an area which likely will accept some HRD odor from an adjoining area due to wind conditions. In the law enforcement field, the best practice is that the K9 must not locate (or alert to) animal remain distracters. Therefore, putting animal remains in the testing area is very important.

4. When placing a subject into the woods for a wilderness air scent test in a 40-60 acre area, be aware of wind conditions and the direction of the wind placing the person in an area conducive to air scenting. Do not use a hot track (trail) allowing the dog to trail to the person. Set the victim in place from another portion of the search area so the dog begins the exercise/test without the scent of a human in the start area.

5. Select a subject that has not hidden for the air scent dog. For an HRD test, try to obtain a variety of materials so that you are not using the same exact human remains materials that the dog trains with on a weekly basis. In the law enforcement field, the best practice is that the materials used in testing are different than those used in training.

6. Tell the handler what the parameters of the search are and what is out of bounds. Review the testing criteria, timing allowed, breaks allowed (whether this counts toward the time or not), description of the missing subject (in an air scent

problem), how many HRD source aides are hidden (if that is allowed), and any other pertinent information before beginning the problem. Be sure the handler has and carries all the required equipment and/or supplies that the test requires. In the law enforcement field, the best practice is that the handler does not know if the search area is negative / blank (no target) or how many target odors are placed there.

7. Give the handler a map of the search area and ask them to locate themselves on the map (which should be part of the testing requirements. If a K9 team finds someone or something, they must be able to tell law enforcement where it is.)

8. Ask the handler to describe their search strategy and scent conditions...and / or scent theory as applicable to the environment (if a part of the test). Note the time of the beginning of the test after all discussion has ended.

During the actual test:

9. Keep your eyes focused on either the handler or the dog. Be mindful of looking in the direction of the hidden subject.

10. Avoid pointing or otherwise indicating the location of the subject.

11. Keep a constant pace and distance behind the dog handler. Do not speed up to "catch up" when the handler begins to approach the subject so you can see adequately to evaluate the alert/indication and/or refind. Instead position yourself at all times so you can observe the handler and dog.

12. Avoid eating or drinking (other than water) to avoid distracting the dog.

13. Avoid talking or directing the dog in any way. No petting or praise.

14. Avoid answering any questions from the handler which may inadvertently provide additional information on where the subject is located. All questions should be asked prior to beginning the exercise. Any questions asked by the handler during the testing should only pertain to information which will not assist the handler or dog in any form or fashion during their quest to locate the missing subject.

15. Decide ahead of time whether the handler may confirm or deny a handler's decision to say that a source material is located "here." Some evaluators will confirm each location (as a false indication and a call by the handler will then terminate the test if no negative/false indications are allowed.) Other agencies will neither confirm nor deny until the test is complete.

16. Evaluators should avoid idle chatter or a discussion of the search techniques of the handler. They should also not offer suggestions or helpful hints to the handler. This can be extremely disturbing to the handler who is already under stress during the testing conditions.

17. When the evaluators have determined that ample time has passed, the handler has located all the items needed to pass the test, weather conditions deteriorate such that it is no longer safe to continue the test, or for some other reason the test is concluded, officially note the time of the end of the test.

After the test has ended:

18. If there are multiple evaluators, quietly and away from the handler and dog, determine the success or failure of the test prior to advising the handler of their pass/fail status. It is usually more effective to have a pass/fail...not a grading situation or other point system. If one of those is used, avoid providing those results to the handler, but instead just provide a pass or fail indication. (Invariably multiple handlers will not be able to agree on how many points for each criteria but if the testing criteria is clear...i.e. the handler must.... And the dog must....it is usually a clear decision as to whether the dog did or did not find, alert, and the handler identify the location, direct the dog, etc.

19. After the test is complete, it is acceptable to provide positive feedback or suggestions for future training goals, whether the handler has passed or failed.

20. Remember that testing is stressful no matter how prepared you may be. No one wants to fail, but a handler and/or dog which is not prepared or able to successfully complete the testing criteria should not be passed or certified. This would be the biggest disservice that one could bestow upon the handler / dog team and outright dishonest. However, be gentle and suggestive of what future training skills may be needed to become successful in a kind and compassionate manner. Be gentle, failure hurts.

21. Once the test is completed and the candidate has successfully passed the certification criteria, congratulate the dog handler and dog. Provide them with a written documentation they can take with them showing their successful completion of the test. Either pre-prepare or send the handler a professional certificate documenting their successful completion of the test complete with an expiration date. If the agency has determined that testing every year is appropriate or testing every two years is appropriate, state that expiration date on their completion certificate. One test is never adequate for an entire SAR career.

22. Document in your personal records that you have tested the dog/handler and the results of that testing.

## Ethics

Much can and has been written about ethics in search and rescue. General ethical behavior applies as much to this job as anywhere else. If you would not do it at your place of employment, do not do it during a training or search mission. If you cannot do it in front of a law enforcement officer, do not do it at all.

- Always behave, train, certify, and respond in a professional manner.

- Avoid bringing any human remains training aids on the scene of a real search. One exception would be a large area or long mission, where a third-party (I recommend law enforcement) would put out a motivational find for the dog. Then the find would be removed from the area by the third party.

- Always keep accurate and up-to-date logs and search reports.

- Strive to read and/or attend training seminars and conferences to be up-to-date on the latest search and rescue trends, training, and search techniques.

- Avoid those who self-deploy and never self-deploy yourself or your dog.

- Do not hold yourself or your dog out to be more than what you are which means do not respond to any request or search that you are not qualified and trained to do based upon your training, certification, and search experiences.  Do not deploy your dog if the dog is not appropriately certified according to written standards.

▪ Do not associate with or participate in fund-raising activities for you, your dog, your team or anyone else who is not a legitimate, legal, responding entity or agency. This means that the agency or team adheres to standards, are reliable, trains regularly, certifies appropriately, and maximizes their skills based upon a recognized curriculum, standard or documented operating procedures.

▪ It must be written down to be recognized.  In Court, if it is not documented, it did not happen.

▪ Respond and participate in search and rescue operations based upon the right reasons.  This is not a time for self-promotion, acting or promoting yourself or your dog as a hero, or for other self-promotional reasons.  There is one reason for SAR...that is to locate the missing person.  Remember that mission.

▪ It is not up to you to determine whether the remains are there or not, whether to bring in the tractor, close off an area, or anything else other than to work your dog in the area where you are assigned.  Your job is to work your dog to the best of your ability based upon conditions and report back to appropriate personnel what changes in behavior you observed in your dog; nothing more, nothing less.

## The Courtroom

Terry Fleck, noted expert and advisor in police dog and handler courtroom testimony and evidence, suggests that:

"Federal and state case law state that when one of these types of dogs (search and rescue, trailing, tracking, scent identification dog, etc.) alerts to or locates human odor, that alert is only one reasonable suspicion indicator. Reasonable suspicion is defined as a particularized and objective basis for suspected legal wrong-doing"[26]

Since the dog alert is only one indicator, the law enforcement officer will need to develop other indicators to achieve probable cause. (Probably cause is when a reasonable person would believe that with a fair probability the defendant has committed a crime.) In other words, "the dog alert must be corroborated by other evidence."[27] (This is relevant in order to obtain a search warrant or arrest the suspected criminal.)

In addition, in the courtroom, the three legal principals of trained, certified and reliable must be proven in order to admit the testimony. Are there adequate training logs which show ongoing training? Has the dog been tested to a set of standards which are similar or equal to national organizations or certified by a national organization (most would suggest within the last one year)? Is the dog reliable in alerting only on human remains (to the exclusion of animal bones, animal remains and/or other distracters, such as food? In order to admit any testimony or evidence, the handler must meet all three of these legal principals.

Adding to those three principals...the handler must show that the dog is of a recognized breed or mix which can reasonably be expected to work off lead. The dog must also be able to differentiate between human and animal scent. There should have been no alerting on animal remains in training or on previous searches. These factors help to provide information as to the credibility and ability of the dog to be able to perform cadaver searches. In addition, the dog should have a history of finding human remains in training and previous searches (if applicable.) Training records should show various training scenarios over the course of the training. Reliability is also of concern and records and training should show no previous false alerts...or training plans which suggest this has been corrected if a problem in the past (problems identified and solved). This proves that the dog is qualified to search for human remains.

Note that in 2013 there was a United States Supreme Court Case which ultimately allowed evidence by a police dog that was not up to date on his logs (produced no logs) and was currently out-of-date with his certification (over a year late). The evidence was allowed into court. This case alone, will strongly affect future court cases involving police dogs, and ultimately search dogs. For a more detailed explanation of legalities

---

[26] Fleck, Terry. Cadaver Dog's alert as Reasonable Suspicion, not Probable Cause.
http://www.policek9.com/Fleck/Cadaver%20Dogs.pdf P. 1 of 6.
[27] IBID. P. 1.

involved in search and rescue, please consult the How to Train a Human Remains Detection Dog, and legal updates provided by Terry Fleck such as information regarding Florida vs. Harris.[28] Handlers are expected to stay attuned to the latest developments in the legal world and national protocols in order to continue getting callouts from law enforcement agencies. It is critical they are informed and up to date.

While the legalities are unclear as to whether the cadaver dog is regarded as a Contraband Substance dog or a Human Scent dog, the author is unaware of any case law allowing a cadaver dog alert to be probable cause; it is considered reasonable suspicion only. (If the cadaver dog were classified into the Contraband Substance dog category, the alert would be considered probable cause; however, this is not yet the case.)

All teams and individuals should understand and research any related data regarding the use of dog testimony in court cases since you may find yourself in that witness stand at some point in your career. Note to self: Just a few short years ago the first federal murder case was prosecuted finding the two defendants guilty. They are now on death row. A SAR team chief was subpoenaed to testify in this case even though the dogs on the team did not locate the body. His testimony included mitigation information in the penalty phase of the case. Stranger things have happened. Understand your participation in the legal process. If in doubt, ask an old-timer, and trust your dog!

Terry Fleck, noted expert, recommends that any evidence located in a search, be recovered by law enforcement. The handler simply reports to his law enforcement liaison what the dog alerted to, located, etc. Law enforcement should then handle the recovery. Be sure to ask directions from your local law enforcement personnel before completing your mission briefing…and follow their instructions.

Remember…ignorance of the law is not excuse. You must be more than aware and informed of standard protocol. You must follow it. In conclusion, when you have a question about training, logs, ethics, the court system, or anything else in SAR, ask your team. Ask your mentors. Consult with law enforcement. There are lots of folks out there with many, many years of experience who will be happy to help guide and mentor you. Find a good one and appreciate him or her.

Handlers working Human Remains Detection dogs, which may be cross-trained or single-purpose dogs, are highly recommended to read the entire Legalities chapter in the

---

[28] Florida vs. Harris United States Supreme Court Decision. http://www.supremecourt.gov/opinions/12pdf/11-817_5if6.pdf

Training a Human Remains Detection Dog, co-authored by the writer of this text. It provides much detail and preparation for the handler who will be testifying in court. Since most live finds are not criminal cases (although some certainly can be), that information is not included in this book. This author recommends all handlers keep training records, search reports, and certification documents to support their training and expertise. Rather prepared than a liability in the court case. What a shame for evidence to be dismissed as a result of an ill-prepared handler. Be prepared.

Stay safe and happy training.

May God bless and keep each of you safe
    as you give so much of yourselves to the family and missing person.
    Your quest is truly admirable and your actions memorable. You matter.
    Kiss your dog goodnight and sleep well.

# Appendix

**Resources:**

The Canine Legal Update and Opinions Web Site at www.k9fleck.org, authored by Terry Fleck, will provide current K9 legality information, case law and tactics.

Search and Rescue (SAR), Tracking and Cadaver K9 Personnel

If you work with Search and Rescue, Tracking and/or Cadaver K9s, your web site membership grants you access to the Search and Rescue / Cadaver K9 areas, the law enforcement Tracking/Trailing areas, along with K9 articles, K9 resources, and exclusive member phone and email support, provided by Terry Fleck, Subject Matter Expert (SME) on SAR, Tracking and Cadaver K9.
Contact Terry at terry@k9fleck.org

Also included in this appendix:

Forms and information which may be helpful when handling a search and rescue dog...training and searches.

# Sample Canine Evaluation Form

_____ Team Canine Evaluation Form

**Handler:**_____

**Canine:**_____

Date of Test: _____

**Status:** Yes: Met Standard     **No**: Did Not Meet Standard     **NA**: not applicable___

Records Produced:___Immunization Records___ Training Logs (length of time:_____)

## Obedience:

| Item | Status | Item | Status |
|---|---|---|---|
| Approaching Strangers | | Eagerness to Work | |
| Responsive to handler off lead | | Recall from group of K9's | |
| Recall from distractions | | Another handler can handle | |
| K9Loads with other K9's | | Jump/Load into Truck | |
| Cross a stream | | Jump One Jump | |
| Walk Catwalk | | Ride Quietly in Vehicle | |
| Enter/Exit Vehicle | | Heal on lead | |
| One Minute Sit | | Three Minute Down | |
| Stand for Exam | | Come/distance 20 Ft | |
| No aggression | | CGC TEST | |

## Wilderness/Area Missing Person Search:

| Item | Status | Item | Status |
|---|---|---|---|
| Finds one victim in 40 acres | | Refind | |
| Indicates to Handler o find | | Reasonable Amt of Time | |
| Search Strategy Described | | Handler Describes Alert | |
| Describes Scent Theory | | Follows Search Strategy | |
| **Pass/Did Not Pass:** Signature of Evaluator | | Date | |
| Signature of Observer | | Date | |
| Signature of K9 Handler | | Date | |
| Signature of Missing Subject | | Date | |

## Tracking/Trailing- Type III:

| DOT | Item | Status | DOT | Item | Status |
|---|---|---|---|---|---|
| | Trail 1/4 - 1/2 mile; aged 4 hrs | | | trail with 2 recent cross tracks | |
| | one turn in the trail | | | more than one terrain feature | |
| | min 15 min/max two hours | | | establish dir. of travel | |
| | dir. of travel in contaminated area | | | uncontaminated scent article | |

## Pass/Did Not Pass:

| | | |
|---|---|---|
| Signature of Evaluator | Date | |
| Signature of Observer | Date | |
| Signature of K9 handler | Date | |

## Cadaver - Land:

| Item | Status | Item | Status |
|---|---|---|---|
| Operational Wilderness | | On lead/off lead | |
| one acre area | | No false indications | |
| Obvious K9 indication/alert | | Reasonable amount of time | |
| Handler describes search strategy | | Two out of three samples found | |
| One sample buried 4 - 6 inches | | One sample buried 10-12 inches | |
| One sample suspended | | One sample under brush/field | |

**Pass/Did Not Pass:**

| | | |
|---|---|---|
| Signature of Evaluator | Date | |
| Signature of Observer | Date | |
| Signature of K9 Handler | Date | |

**Comments:**

# SAR Canine Training Log

K9:_____Handler:_____
Date:_____        _____
Location:_____
Mileage: Beginning:_____Ending:_____Total:_____
Beginning Time: _____ Ending Time:_____ Total:_____

## Conditions:
Wind Speed:_____ Wind Direction:_____ Humidity:_____ Temperature:_____
Cloud Cover:_____ Shadow (ft): _____ Other:_____
Rain:__  Hail:__  Snow:__  Sleet: __  Other:_____

## Environment:
___Grass            ___Brush          ___Timber          ___Level
___Rolling          ___Steep          ___Thick           ___Thin
___Moderate         ___Rubble         ___Ext. Building   ___Residential
___Clpsed Structure ___Inter. Bld.    ___Commercial      ___Industrial
___Lake             ___Pond           ___River           ___Creek
___From boat        ___From Shore

_____
_____
_____

**Size of Search Area/Length of Trail:**_____

**Age of Exercise** (i.e. hrs, days, etc):_____
**Scent Article Used**:_____**Age of Scent Article:**_____

## Type of Exercise/Training:
___Agility           ___Directional      ___Obedience
___Socialization     ___Area Search      ___Area Search w/ Pop-Up
___Runaway reps      ___Trail            ___Area Search w/ Callout
___HRD               ___Water Recovery   ___Disaster
___ Indication/Alert

## Training Subjects:
___Location Known to handler          ___ Location Unknown to Handler

156

___Live/Mobile      ___Live/Immobile      ___Live/Concealed
___Live/Bizarre Behavior

Victim Description:  ____Age          _____Race          ____Weight
                     ____Gender       ____ Height        _____Other

**HRD:**
___HRD / Visible____HRD / Concealed____HRD / Overhead_____HRD / Buried

**HRD Sample Type/Age:**
_____

Sketch of Search Area and Exercise:

Notes:

# Lost Person Questionnaire - _____ <u>COMPREHENSIVE</u>

NOTE: Use pencil/black ink, print clearly. Avoid confusing phrases/words and unfamiliar abbreviations. Complete and detail answers for future use. Answer ALL questions, if possible.

Incident Title: _____ Today's date: _____ Time: _____
Interviewer(s): _____ Incident number: _____

## A. SOURCE(S) OF INFORMATION FOR QUESTIONNAIRE

Name: _____ How Info Taken: _____
Home Address: _____
Phone 1: _____ Phone 2: _____ Relationship: _____
Where/How to contact now: _____
Where/How to contact later: _____
What does informant believe happened: _____

## B. LOST PERSON

Full Name: _____ DOB: _____ Sex: _____
Maiden Name: _____ Nicknames: _____ Other AKA's: _____
Home Address: _____ Zip: _____
Local Address: _____ Zip: _____
Home Phone: _____ Local Phone: _____ E-mail Address_____
Birthplace: _____ Ethnicity: _____ National Origin: _____ Language Spoken: ____

## C. PHYSICAL DESCRIPTION

Height: _____ Weight: _____ Age: _____ Build: _____ Eye Color: __
Hair: Color Current: _____ Natural: _____ Length: _____ Style/Binding: _____ Wig: _
　　　Beard: _____ Style/Color _____ Mustache: ____ Style/Color _____ Sideburns: ___
Facial features shape: _____ Skin color: _____ Tone: _____ Complexion:__
Color of fingernails: _____ Fake nails: _____ Color of finger nails: _____
Distinguishing marks (scars/moles/tattoos/piercing): _____
Jewelry (and where worn, incl. Medical bracelets); _____
Eyewear/Contacts (sunglasses, spares): _____ Eyesight w/out glasses: _____
Overall Appearance: _____
Photo Available: Y _ N _ Where: _____ Need to be returned: Y _
Comments: _____
_____

## D. TRIP PLANS OF SUBJECT

Started from: _____ Day/Date:_____ Time: _____

Going to: _____ Via: _____

Purpose: _____

For how long?_____ Exit date: _____ Alone? Y __ N ___ Group size: _____

Done trip before? Y __ N ___ Details: _____

Transported by whom/means: _____

Vehicle now located at: _____ Type:_____ Color: _____

    License #: _____ State: _____ Verified? Y __ N __ By whom: _____

Return time: _____ From where: _____

    By whom/what: _____

Additional names, cars, licenses, etc. for party: _____

Alternate                  plans/routes/objectives                discussed:

_____

Discussed with whom: _____ When: _____

Comments: _____

_____

## E. CLOTHING

|  | STYLE | COLOR | SIZE | OTHER |
|---|---|---|---|---|
| Shirt sweater: |  |  |  |  |
| Pants (belt/suspenders): |  |  |  |  |
| Outerwear: |  |  |  |  |
| Under wear/socks: |  |  |  |  |
| Head wear: |  |  |  |  |
| Rain wear: |  |  |  |  |
| Glasses: |  |  |  |  |
| Gloves: |  |  |  |  |
| Neck ware (scarf/neckerchief/tie): |  |  |  |  |
| Extra clothing: |  |  |  |  |
| Footwear: |  |  |  |  |

    Sole type: _____ Sample available? Y __ N ___ Where: _____

Scent articles available? Y __ N __ What: _____ Secured?: Y __

Where         is        scent        article        now?

Overall _____ coloration _____ as _____ seen _____ from _____ air:
_____

**F. LAST SEEN**
Time: _____ Where:_____ Why/how: _____
Seen by whom: _____ Location now: _____
Who last talked at length with person: _____
    Where: _____ Subject matter: _____
Weather at time: _____ Weather since: _____
Seen going which way: _____ When: _____
Reason for leaving: _____
Attitude (confident, confused, etc.): _____
Subject complaining of anything: _____
Subject seem tired: _____ Cold/Hot:_____ Other: _____
Comments: _____
_____

**G. OUTDOOR EXPERIENCE**

Familiar with area? Y ___ N ___ How Recent: _____ Other: _____
Other areas of travel: _____
Formal outdoor training / degree: _____
    Where: _____ When: _____
Medical training: _____ When: _____
Scouting experience: _____ When:_____ Where: _____
    How much: _____ Scout rank: _____ Scout Leader?: Y _
Military Experience? Y _ N __ What: _____ When: _____
Where: _____ Rank: _____Other: _____
Generalized previous experience: _____
How much overnight experience: _____
Ever lost before? Y ___ N ___ Where: _____ When: _____
Ever go out alone? Y _ N __
Where: _____
Stay on trail or cross country: _____
How fast does subject hike: _____
Athletic/other interests: _____
Climbing experience: _____
Comments: _____

**H. HABITS / PERSONALITY**

Smoke? Y _____ N _____ How Often: _____ What: _____ Brand: _____
Alcohol? Y ___ N _____ How Often: _____ What: _____ Brand: _____
Recreational drugs? Y __ N ____ What: _____

Gum brand: _____ Candy brand: _____ Other: _____

Hobbies/Interests: _____

Outgoing / quiet: _____ Gregarious / loner: _____

Evidence of leadership: _____ Give up easy / Keep going: _____

Legal trouble (past I present): _____

Hitchhike? Y ___ N __ Accepts rides easily: _____

Personal problems: _____

Religious? Y ___ N __ Faith: _____ To what degree: _____

Personal values: _____

Philosophy: _____

Person closest to: _____ In family: _____

Emotional history: _____

Education Highest grade achieved: ___ Current status: _____ College Education: _____

    School name: _____

    Teachers: _____

    Subject/Degree: _____ Year: _____

Local/fictional hero: _____

Comments: _____

## I. HEALTH / GENERAL CONDITION

Overall health: _____

Overall physical condition: _____

Known medical/dental problems: _____

    Knowledgeable doctor: _____ Phone: _____

Handicaps/deformities/prosthetics: _____

Known psychological problems: _____

    Knowledgeable person: _____ Phone: _____

Medication: _____

    Dosages: _____

    Knowledgeable person: _____ Phone: _____

What will happen without meds: _____

Dentures/Partials: _____ Dentist: _____ Phone: _____

Comments: _____

_____

## J. EQUIPMENT

|  | *STYLE* | *COLOR* | *BRAND* | *SIZE* |
|---|---|---|---|---|
| Pack: | | | | |
| Tent: | | | | |
| Sleeping Bag: | | | | |
| Ground Cloth/Pad: | | | | |
| Fishing Equipment: | | | | |
| Climbing Equipment: | | | | |
| Light: | | | | |
| Knife: | | | | |
| Camera: | | | | |

Stove: _____ Fuel: _____ Starter Y __ N __ What: _____

Drinking Liquid Container: _____ Liquid Amount: _____ Kind of Liquid: __

Compass: _____ Map: _____ Of Where: _____

How Competent with Map/Compass: _____

Food: _____

Brands: _____

Skis: Type: _____ Brand:_____ Color: _____ Size: _____

    Bindings: _____ Pole Type:_____ Length: _____

    How Competent: _____

Snowshoes: Type: _____ Brand:_____ Color: _____ Size: _____

    Bindings: _____ How Competent:_____

Firearms: Y __ N ___ Brand: _____ Model: _____ Holster: _____

Money: Amount: _____ Credit/Debit Cards: _____

Other Documents: _____

Comments: _____

## K. CONTACTS PERSON WOULD MAKE UPON REACHING CIVILIZATION

Full Name: _____ Relationship: _____

Address: _____ Zip: _____

Phone #: _____ Anyone Home Now? Y _

**L. CHILDREN**

Afraid of the dark? Y  N      Animals? Y  N      Afraid                                    of:
_____
Feelings toward adults: _____  Strangers: _____
Reactions when hurt: _____  Cry: _____
Training when lost: _____
Active/lethargic/antisocial: _____
Comments: _____
_____

**M. GROUPS OVERDUE**

Name/Kind of group: _____  Leader: _____
Experience of group leader: _____
Address/Phone of knowledgeable person: _____
Personality clashes within group: _____
Leader types in group other than leader: _____
What would subject do if separated from group: _____
Competitive spirit of group: _____
Intergroup dynamics: _____
Comments: _____
_____

**N. ACTIONS TAKEN SO FAR**

By: Family/Friends: _____
Results:
_____
Others:
_____
Results:
_____
Comments: _____
_____

**0. PRESS/FAMILY RELATIONS**

Next of kin: _____  Relationship: _____
Address: _____  Zip: _____
Phone #: _____  Occupation: _____

Significant family problems: _____

Family's desire to employ special assistance: _____

Comments: _____

_____

**P. OTHER INFORMATION (Use back of form)**

_____

_____

Additional Notes:

## What to Do When You Arrive on Scene....

Tune to your team pre-determined radio channel.

1. Break your dog in an out of the way spot and pick up any waste.

2. Determine the location of your team meeting place/parking area.

3. Determine location of the command post.

4. Check in with your team leader and sign in to command center or base of operations.
   It is helpful to present an ID card with your photo and pertinent emergency information about whom to contact in case of an accident or emergency.

5. Your team chief or other individual/operations chief will provide you with a briefing of the incident and pertinent information and instructions or an assignment.
   Questions about procedures? What should you do if you discover a clue?
   The    weapon? The body? The missing person? Just ask.

6. Proceed to prepare to execute the assignment given.

7. During your assignment...mission:

   KEEP good notes while in the field. What do you do precisely? How did you search the area? Who was on your search crew? Who gave you the assignment? What you found, did not find, etc.? What areas you covered? What areas were not covered and why? Recommendations for further searching? Hazards encountered? This is the type of information that should go into your PERSONAL search report. Your personal search report is forwarded to the chief of the team after the search and on file with the search documents.

   Once you turn in your personal search report, you may THEN be forwarded a copy of the team report which the team leader or chief will provide.

   NOTE: If you are asked to be the documentation for your search crew, this means you are taking notes for everyone on the team and will need to provide a copy to all crew members so they can complete their own report either before leaving the site or directly upon arrival home via email.   Before giving anyone a copy of YOUR notes on the scene (or before you leave) it is YOUR responsibility to make a copy so you will have all that info for your personal report.

All searches are a bit different.  Adapt to the circumstances.

Remember:  If YOU are the first person on scene, YOU begin the sign in sheets.  IF you do not have a to-go packet in your car (complete with copies of all the standard SAR forms), you are behind the eight ball and need to get one organized.  WE are all in  charge of documentation.

8.  Upon completion of your assignment, report back to the command center to de-brief and submit your search findings.  Receive another assignment or sign out to leave the scene.

9.  Return home and upon returning home, immediately wash your uniform, re-pack for the next callout, decontaminate your dog if needed, and remember to listen to your significant other about the important events of their day.  It makes for a good relationship in the long run.

10. Complete your individual search report as soon as possible and within 48 hours while the search is still fresh on your mind.  Submit your personal report to your team chief who will in turn use all the individual reports to create a team final report which is often submitted to the lead detective of the sheriff department or police department heading up the search activities.

11. Refer to the chapter on Critical Incident Stress Debriefing if the search included a death of any sort...or any other traumatic event.

12. Take care of you...shower, stress-less activity such as watching television, good meal, and good company.  Revel in the fact that you did a good job and helped another family in need.  Pat yourself on your back, quietly and secretly, smile, and continue living your life as usual.

## Sample Search Report

**_____Search and Rescue Team**

Name, Date and Location

1. Notification procedure, date and time:

2. Met team members at _____, time, and place.

3. Arrived on scene (address, etc.) at _____ (time). Address of missing person home/place last seen. (Miles driven, general description of how to get to the base of operations.)

4. Missing Person Description: (age, race, height, weight, hair/eye color, clothing, etc.)

5. Briefing information about the case: (what were you told about the case by the search manager and/or official briefing...not general conversation; Alzheimer's, medications, etc.)

6. Weather, conditions, hazards: temperature, humidity (raining, etc.), wind conditions, snakes, ticks, etc.

7. Place last seen: address or description

8. Time last seen:

9. Assignment 1:
    Time out:        Time Back in:
    Assignment:
    Task Completed:
    Results:

Assignment 2:

Assignment 3:

10. Signed out of search location/base of operations at _____.

11. Debriefing attended: (location, time, etc.)

12. Results of Debriefing:

13. Final disposition of search? (Found alive, located 3 wks later, still missing, etc.) – You may add this at a later time.

14. Arrived home at: (time)

Other information

1. Facts only. We are not investigators. We are searchers doing a job as requested by LEO.

2. Report all clues located with a detailed description of what was found and exact location using UTM's. Pictures, if possible. Don't touch, ever. Follow command instructions...either flag or bag.

3. If using a map, use topographical maps with exact coordinates. If using other types of maps, indicate exact locations using UTM's and the map datum that matches the map you were using. If the map datum is unknown, use NAD 27 as your default map datum.

4. Always follow and complete the paperwork trail....

   a. Assignment Sheet - one per assignment.

   b. Each individual searcher keeps his own personal notes in the field. If you are asked to document while on a mission, those are given to the crew leader at the end of each assignment...you should keep a copy for your own notes.

   c. Debriefing form reporting back to the search manager, in writing, before receiving your next assignment. Each assignment. This is done in detail.

   d. Team debriefing...usually held directly after the search at a neutral location away from the BOO (Base of Operation). Review of ops and check with each individual to determine safety status to return home. (Example...too tired to drive home safely, disturbed about the search operations, discussions of what went well and what needs improvement next time, etc.)

e. Turn in search report within 48 hours...preferably within 24 hours so a team report can be completed and sent to LEO. This is not as detailed as individual reports. The search manager prepares the team report which goes to LEO. Individual reports are turned in to the team Chief who uses this info to prepare the team overview.

# How to Collect an Uncontaminated Scent Article
## (When working a scent specific air scent or trailing dog)

Written by Nancy Culberson, NC

The "Scent Article Collection Bag" has the things you may need to collect/make scent articles. It has *plastic/locking* bags, gauze pads, gloves, and a marker to write down information about the collection of the scent article.

A 2 gallon *locking* bag easily holds the following materials:

### Scent Article Collection Bag
2 Pairs latex gloves
5 Gauze pads
5 Pint size *freezer bags*
*2 Quart size freezer bags*
*1 Gallon size freezer bag*
1 *permanent* marker

A "Large" bag has 10 ea. – gauze pads and pint size bags.

Information to write on Scent Bags containing collected scent articles:

Subject: _____
Date: _____ Time: _____
Collector: _____
Known contaminates: _____
_____
Article used for scent: _____
_____
Where article was obtained: _____
_____

**How to use the collection bag –**

1. Open the collection bag and remove the glove bag (which is taped near top of bag to help reduce contamination).
2. Put on gloves. (Use the bag they came out of for trash).
3. Remove Gallon size *freezer* bag.
4. Take out quart size bag containing the gauze pads.
5. Place gauze pads on/in subject's scent article.
6. While gauze pads are absorbing scent, take out quart size bag of pint size *freezer* bags.
7. From the Gallon bag, take out the *permanent* marker.
8. Using the *permanent* marker, fill out the label on the pint size bags.
9. After filling out labels, place the gauze scent articles inside the pint bags.
10. Place the pint bags inside the Gallon bag to give to the IC.

If you'd like to take the original scent article to the Incident Command Post (in case more scent articles need to be created), place it in the 2 gallon Scent Article Collection bag. Write on the outside of the bag all the information that was written on the pint size bags.

**Reminders and suggestions related to scent articles –**

- To reduce contamination, only one person (with gloves on) should be reaching into the bag *that* contains scent article bags. It's preferable if the person is a command staff person, not going out on the search. Again, this minimizes some problems with scent contamination.

- The K9 handler should consider re-bagging the article (if *he/she was* not the original collector). This *helps* to reduce scent transfer from the *collector to the* person distributing the scent *articles.*

- NEVER handle a subject's article with your bare hands. Always wear clean gloves and when possible use a coat hanger/tongs/tweezers *to pick up the article.*

- NEVER use green, black, or white garbage bags to collect or store scent articles, they are usually chemically treated to kill/control odors. Use clean, clear *food-grade freezer bags when possible.*

- Once a K9 team has used a scent article, it should not be used by any other team (since the article now has the scent of the previous K9 team on it).

- Think, think, think about possible cross-contaminations while collecting scent articles.

  ➤ Clothes hampers usually contain multiple family members scent.

  ➤ If collecting scent from a bed, ask if the subject was the only one to ever sleep there *and when the linens were last changed.*

  ➤ Dressers and clothes *hung in closets*– the clothes have usually been washed. *Although the scent would be aged, another source might be items which are not washed regularly and worn more than once, such as a suit jacket.*

  ➤ Socks could have been worn around the house, picking up other household members scent.

  ➤ When collecting *a scent article* from a vehicle, *determine if* the local authorities *entered* the vehicle? Sat down? What did they touch? Who else entered the vehicle? Sometimes it's a good idea to have anyone who entered the *vehicle present* so the K9's can eliminate *that* scent.

## Methods of Using and Collecting Scent –

1. Direct – Let the K9 smell the subjects' article/source directly. Direct scenting poses the greatest risk of contaminating or destroying forensic evidence that could be collected for later investigation.

2. Swiping – Wiping the surface of the article with a sterile gauze pad and transfer the human scent from the source to the pad. The pad is then placed in a bag and later used by the K9 handler to scent their K9. Unfortunately this method can remove or contaminate fingerprints, DNA, or trace evidence.

3. Absorption/passive transfer – Place a sterile gauze pad on the surface or inside the article/source (something that was directly next to the subject skin is best). The pad is left in place for 10 to 20 minutes. Some people like to use the collection baggie to make a mock tent over the article to help condense/trap the scent. Again, the pad is placed inside a *freezer* bag for later use by a K9 handler. This method *is* time consuming.

# CONSENT AND RELEASE FOR PLACENTA DONATION

Team: _____ Team
Address:
Phone:
Name:          _____, Chief


I, _____, the undersigned birth mother of a child born alive, acknowledge that I am over the age of 18 years and am capable of consenting to the donation of Placenta from my body.

I hereby release and donate to _____Search and Rescue the Placenta to be used as a training aid for Human Remains Detection canines.

I agree to make this donation on the condition that I am not to be held responsible for any disease or hazard associated with the use or handling of this Placenta.

In turn, the _____K9 unit agrees that the organization will not hold the undersigned or any medical staff or hospital responsible for any hazard resulting in the use of this tissue.

All Bio-Hazard protocol and handling standards will be observed and instituted.



Signatures:
_____ Date_____
Mother


_____ Date_____
Witness


_____ Date _____
Witness

# CONSENT AND RELEASE FOR TEETH & TISSUE DONATION

Team: _____ Team

Address:
Phone:

Name: _____, Chief

I, _____, acknowledge that I am over the age of 18 years and am capable of consenting to the donation of tissue and teeth from my body.

I hereby release and donate to the _____ Search and Rescue Team the Tissue and Teeth to be used as training aids for Human Remains Detection canines.

I agree to make this donation on the condition that I am not to be held responsible for any disease or hazard associated with the use or handling of this tissue and teeth.

In turn, _____ members agree that the organization will not hold the undersigned or any medical staff or hospital responsible for any hazard resulting in the use of this tissue.

All Bio-Hazard protocol and handling standards will be observed and instituted.

_____
Date_____
Donor Signature

_____
Date_____
Witness Signature

_____
Date_____
Witness Signature

# CONSENT AND RELEASE FOR TISSUE, BLOOD and / or FLUIDS DONATION

Team:

Address:
Phone:

Name: _____, Chief




I, _____, acknowledge that I am over the age of 18 years and am capable of consenting to the donation of tissue, blood and / or fluids from my body.

I hereby release and donate to the _____ Search and Rescue Team, tissue, bone, materials / or Fluids to be used as training aids for Human Remains Detection canines.

I agree to make this donation on the condition that I am not to be held responsible for any disease or hazard associated with the use or handling of this tissue.

In turn, _____ SAR team members agree that the organization will not hold the undersigned or any medical staff or hospital responsible for any hazard resulting in the use of this tissue.

All Bio-Hazard protocol and handling standards will be observed and instituted.


_____          Date _____
Donor


_____          Date_____
Witness


_____          Date _____
Witness

## Suggested Reading

### *More Books by Christy Judah*

*Available at www.christyjudah.com or www.amazon.com*
*christyjudah@gmail.com*

**Search & Rescue Books:**

A Tribute to Search and Rescue Dogs
Building a Basic Foundation for Search and Rescue Dog Training
Building a Search and Rescue Team from the Ground Up
Buzzards and Butterflies:  Human Remains Detection Dogs
Water Search:  Finding Drowned Persons
Search and Rescue Canine Training Log
Search and Rescue Log & Journal
Training a Human Remains Detection Dog (with Trace Sargent)

**Children's Books:**

Meet the Search and Rescue Dog
Meet the Police dog
Meet the Native American Indian
Meet the Pirates

**History Books:**

The Legends of Brunswick County:  Ghosts, Pirates, Indians and Colonial North Carolina
More Legends
Two Faces of Dixie:  Politicians, Plantations & Slaves
A Journey through Sampson County
Sabbath Home Baptist Church:  95 Years of Service
Stedman Baptist Church:  A Centennial Celebration

**Family Genealogy:**

Faircloth Family History:  2013

**Others:**
An Ancient History of Dogs:  Spaniels through the Ages
The English Springer Spaniel Puppy


# And more:

Fundamentals of Search and Rescue by NASAR.
Advanced Search and Rescue (ADSAR) by NASAR.
Scent and the Scenting Dog by William Syrotuck.

- Additional Recommended Reading available at the NASAR book store... www.nasar.org

- Check out more K9 related reading at the Dogwise Book Store: www.dogwise.com


Conclusion:  **Remember...you are a searcher first and a SAR Dog handler second...so prepare yourself to be a top notch searcher.   Tomorrow is another day.  If what you have done today does not work, then try something else tomorrow.**

Trust your dog.

Remember that we search so that others may live.

9-11

We shall never forget!

Figure 63 K9 Cynder.  Handler:  Pam Bennett.

Figure 64 K9 Storm.  Handler: Jim Ware.

*Happiness comes of the capacity to feel deeply, to enjoy simply, to think freely*
*to risk life, to be needed.*
**Storm Jameson**

*Depend not on another, but lean instead on thyself...*
*True happiness is born of self-reliance.*
**The Laws of Manu**

Printed in the United States of America.

CPSIA information can be obtained
at www.ICGtesting.com
Printed in the USA
LVOW05s0153050816

499092LV00006BA/269/P

9 781500 141967